100 afghan squares to knit

100 afghan squares to knit

PATTERNS AND INSTRUCTIONS FOR AFGHAN SQUARES FOR BLANKETS AND THROWS

Debbie Abrahams

Trafalgar Square Publishing

I dedicate this book to Heddy, my mother, who worked with unwavering commitment throughout the production of my designs for this book.

First published in the United States of America in 2002 by Trafalgar Square Publishing, North Pomfret, Vermont 05053

9 8 7 6 5 4

ISBN 1-57076-222-8

Library of Congress Catalog Number: 2001098310

EDITOR: Kate Haxell
DESIGNER: Luise Roberts
PHOTOGRAPHER: Jon Bouchier
PATTERN CHECKER: Eva Yates

Reproduction by Classic Scan Pte Ltd, Singapore
Printed and bound by Kyodo Printing Co Pte Ltd, Singapore

Contents

Hand-knitting, for the creative designer, is not only a wonderful way to add to your wardrobe, but it is becoming ever more popular as a means of furnishing your home with uniquely crafted accessories. My intention, through this book, is to produce a range of knitted afghans that use a combination of yarns and decorative embellishments and that, at the same time, allow the knitter to experiment with exciting new ideas. My designs are a far cry from the traditional knitted blankets made up from old gauge squares. A range of different yarns in vibrant shades have been used, including denim, mohair, lurex, wools and cottons, along with brilliantly colored sequins, beads and hand-made buttons. This fusion of colors and textures creates hand-knitted textiles that are appealing to the eye and sympathetic to the touch.

These projects are an invitation to all knitters of varying abilities to pick up their needles and come with me on a creative adventure, discovering the endless opportunities that are offered on these pages. Because each afghan is made up of individual squares, the prospective knitter can take needles and yarns and literally knit anywhere – on the bus, the train, at work or in the home, with each square being worked separately and then later stitched together. There is an opportunity to follow the designs as shown, or if preferred, the knitter can create alternative versions by selecting different squares, by mixing squares taken from various designs, by choosing a personal choice of colors, or by experimenting with a variety of arrangements. Anything is possible!

Debbie Abrahams

How to use this book

Each separate square has full instructions, either in the form of a written pattern or a chart. In addition there is a color photograph of every square, with some squares having additional photographs showing different colorways. Each chart has a key next to it, and below is a summary of the various symbols used, both in the charts and with the patterns. Before you start a square, check to see if it has a chart, a photograph or both.

In addition there is a techniques section starting on page 121 that has step-by-step instructions for intarsia knitting (the technique used for all of the squares), bead and sequin knitting, embroidery and piecing your afghan.

Key

⊞ Square is charted

▣ Square is illustrated with a photograph

□ K on RS, P on WS

⊟ P on RS, K on WS

⊙ Place bead

⊠ Place button

⊡ Lazy Daisy stitch center

⊞⊞⊞⊞ Cable six back

flower power

Being a child of the seventies it was inevitable that I would be aware of the influence of Flower Power. Throughout history painters and designers have used a floral motif in numerous ways, I chose to use it for its connotations of color, serenity and well-being. The traditional custom of giving flowers as a sign of friendship and love is seen by all as a humane, kind gesture and the stylized flower motif that I have developed symbolizes this theme of peace and love. Bright, happy colors are embellished with beads and embroidered stitches that add interest and detail to the overall design. While the flower is a basic repeating shape, variation is introduced through the texture, beads and embroidery. A significant feature of this afghan is the interspersing of vibrant stripes that are mixed with the floral motifs to create a checkerboard effect.

SIZE
75in × 53in (192cm × 134cm)

MATERIALS
1 pair US 5 (3.75mm/No. 9) needles
2 circular US 3 (3.25mm/No. 10)
   needles 39in (100cm) length

Yarn
Rowan Wool Cotton
1¾oz (50g) balls

pale yellow	10
bright orange	5
mid blue	5
royal blue	5
red	4
green	5
magenta	4
mauve	2

Rowan Lurex Shimmer
(used double throughout)
1oz (25g) balls

wine red	2

Quantities given for individual squares are approximate fractions of a ball.

Beads
³⁄₁₆in (5mm) pebble beads

gold	173
blue	22

GAUGE (TENSION)
24 sts and 32 rows to 4in (10cm) measured over patterned stockinette (stocking) stitch using US 5 (3.75mm/No. 9) needles.

NOTE
Single stitch outlines on squares ③ ④ ⑥ and ⑦ can be Swiss-darned after knitting (see page 123).

ABBREVIATIONS
See page 127.

FINISHING
The sizes given for the finished afghan and individual squares are approximate. The number of stitches in a row, and the number of rows in a square differ in some instances. Therefore, when sewing pieces together, ease the extra stitches or extra rows into the adjoining square.

Press the individual squares using a damp cloth and warm iron. Sew the squares together, joining bound (cast) off edge of one square to the cast on edge of the next square, easing in stitches if necessary, to form vertical strips. Sew the vertical strips together, easing in rows if necessary, to create one block.

Edging

MATERIALS

2 circular US 3 (3.25mm/No. 10) needles 39in (100cm) length

Rowan Wool Cotton
1¾oz (50g) balls
- red (A) 4/5
- pale yellow (B) 3/5
- royal blue (C) 4/5

KNIT

With RS facing and using A, pick up and knit 481 sts along the right-hand edge of the afghan.
Beg with a WS row, cont to work in K1, P1 seed (moss) stitch, inc 1 st at each end of all RS rows, and foll the color stripe patt rep:
A, 3 rows; B, 3 rows; C, 2 rows.
With WS facing bind (cast) off knitwise.
Rep for left-hand edge of afghan.
With RS facing and using A, pick up and knit 333 sts along bottom edge of the afghan.
Rep edging as for right-hand and left-hand edges.
Rep for top edge of afghan.
Neatly sew border edges together.

Order of squares

2	1a	4	1b	7	1c	5	1d	2
1b	8b	1c	8a	1d	8b	1a	8a	1b
7	1d	2	1a	3	1b	6	1c	7
1a	8a	1b	8b	1c	8a	1d	8b	1a
6	1c	5	1d	4	1a	3	1b	6
1d	8b	1a	8a	1b	8b	1c	8a	1d
5	1b	3	1c	2	1d	7	1a	5
1c	8a	1d	8b	1a	8a	1b	8b	1c
4	1a	7	1b	6	1c	2	1d	4
1b	8b	1c	8a	1d	8b	1a	8a	1b
3	1d	6	1a	5	1b	4	1c	3
1a	8a	1b	8b	1c	8a	1d	8b	1a
2	1c	4	1d	7	1a	5	1b	2

QUANTITY OF SQUARES

(1) Crazy stripe		
	(1a) First colorway	15
	(1b) Second colorway	15
	(1c) Third colorway	14
	(1d) Fourth colorway	14
(2) Hot flower		7
(3) Exotic flower		5
(4) Psychedelic flower		6
(5) Happy flower		6
(6) Wild flower		5
(7) Textured flower		6
(8) Speckle		
	(8a) First colorway	12
	(8b) Second colorway	12

(1) Crazy stripe

SIZE

6in × 6in (15cm × 15cm)

MATERIALS

1 pair US 5 (3.75mm/No. 9) needles

(1a) First colorway (×15 ▣)
Rowan Wool Cotton
1¾oz (50g) balls
- mid blue (A) 1/6
- bright orange (B) 1/6

(1b) Second colorway (×15 ▣)
Rowan Wool Cotton
1¾oz (50g) balls
- magenta (A) 1/6
- royal blue (B) 1/6

(1c) Third colorway (×14 ▣)
Rowan Wool Cotton
1¾oz (50g) balls
- mauve (A) 1/6
- pale yellow (B) 1/6

(1d) Fourth colorway (×14 ▣)
Rowan Wool Cotton
1¾oz (50g) balls
- red (A) 1/6
- green (B) 1/6

KNIT

Cast on 39 sts using A.
Working in stockinette (stocking) stitch cont in stripe patt rep as folls, beg with a RS row:
ROWS 1-5: A
ROWS 6-9: B
ROWS 10-13: A
Rep rows 6-13, 4 times more
Rep rows 6-9
Purl 1 row B
(50 rows)
Bind (cast) off sts.

❷ Hot flower

□ K on RS, P on WS

SIZE
6in × 6in (15cm × 15cm)

MATERIALS
1 pair US 5 (3.75mm/No. 9) needles

KNIT
Thread 1 bead onto wine red. Cast on 39 sts and work until chart row 50 completed. Bind (cast) off sts.

Single colorway (×7 ⊞ ▣)
Rowan Wool Cotton
1¾oz (50g) balls
□ pale yellow   ⅛
▨ bright orange   ⅙

Rowan Lurex Shimmer
1oz (25g) balls
■ wine red   ¹⁄₂₅

³⁄₁₆in (5mm) pebble beads
◉ gold   1

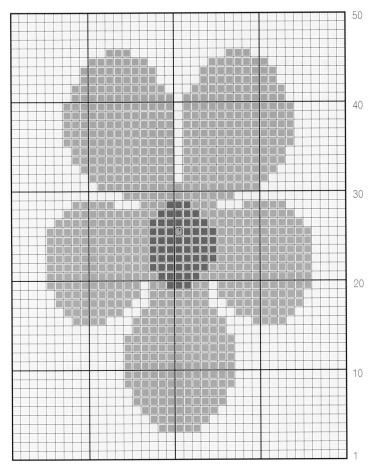

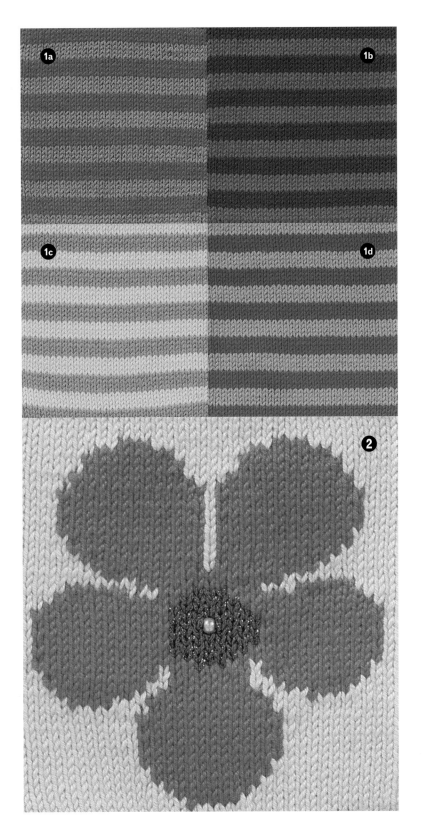

❸ Exotic flower

SIZE
6in × 6in (15cm × 15cm)

MATERIALS
1 pair US 5 (3.75mm/No. 9) needles

Single colorway (×5 ⊞ ▣)
Rowan Wool Cotton
1¾oz (50g) balls

■	royal blue	⅛
■	red	⅙
■	green	1/50

³⁄₁₆in (5mm) pebble beads
⬤ gold   25

☐ K on RS, P on WS

KNIT
Thread 24 beads onto red and
1 bead onto green.
Cast on 39 sts and work until
chart row 50 completed.
Bind (cast) off sts.

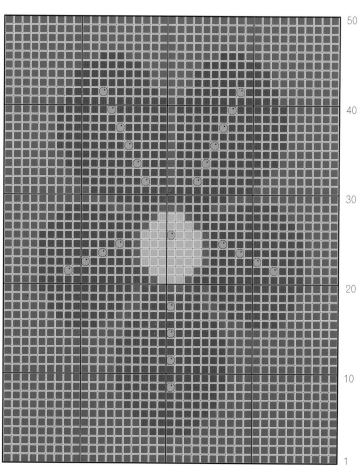

❹ Psychedelic flower

SIZE
6in × 6in (15cm × 15cm)

MATERIALS
1 pair US 5 (3.75mm/No. 9) needles

Single colorway (×6 ⊞ ▣)
Rowan Wool Cotton
1¾oz (50g) balls
▨ bright orange   ⅛
▨ green   ⅙
■ royal blue   1/50

Rowan Lurex Shimmer
1oz (25g) balls
■ wine red   1/25

³⁄₁₆in (5mm) pebble beads
◉ gold   1

☐ K on RS, P on WS

KNIT
Thread 1 bead onto royal blue.
Cast on 39 sts and work until
chart row 50 completed.
Bind (cast) off sts.

❺ Happy flower

SIZE
6in × 6in (15cm × 15cm)

MATERIALS
1 pair US 5 (3.75mm/No. 9) needles

Single colorway (×6 ⊞ ▣)
Rowan Wool Cotton
1¾oz (50g) balls
▨ green   ⅛
■ magenta   ⅙
☐ pale yellow   1/50

³⁄₁₆in (5mm) pebble beads
◉ blue   1

☐ K on RS, P on WS

⊟ P on RS, K on WS

KNIT
Thread 1 bead onto pale yellow.
Cast on 39 sts and work until
chart row 50 completed.
Bind (cast) off sts.

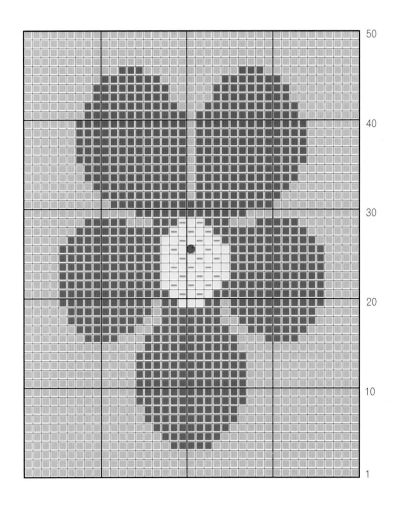

❻ Wild flower

SIZE
6in × 6in (15cm × 15cm)

MATERIALS
1 pair US 5 (3.75mm/No. 9) needles

Single colorway (×5 ⊞ ▣)
Rowan Wool Cotton
1¾oz (50g) balls
▪ magenta   ⅛
▦ mid blue   ⅙
☐ pale yellow   ¹/₂₅

³⁄₁₆in (5mm) pebble beads
◉ gold   8
● blue   1

☐ K on RS, P on WS

KNIT
Thread 4 gold beads, 1 blue bead, then 4 gold beads onto mid blue. Cast on 39 sts and work until chart row 50 completed. Bind (cast) off sts.

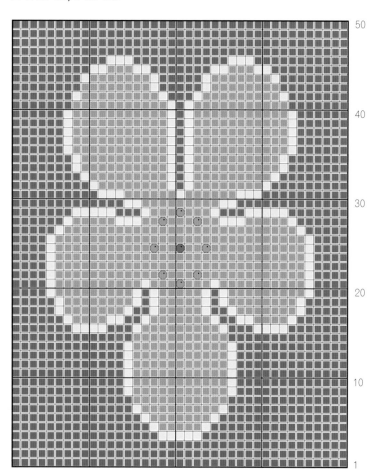

❼ Textured flower

SIZE
6in × 6in (15cm × 15cm)

MATERIALS
1 pair US 5 (3.75mm/No. 9) needles

Single colorway (×6 ⊞ ▣)
Rowan Wool Cotton
1¾oz (50g) balls
▦ mid blue   ⅛
☐ pale yellow   ⅙
▨ green   ¹/₅₀
▪ bright orange   ¹/₅₀

³⁄₁₆in (5mm) pebble beads
● blue   1

☐ K on RS, P on WS

⊟ P on RS, K on WS

KNIT
Thread 1 bead onto green. Cast on 39 sts and work until chart row 50 completed. Bind (cast) off sts.

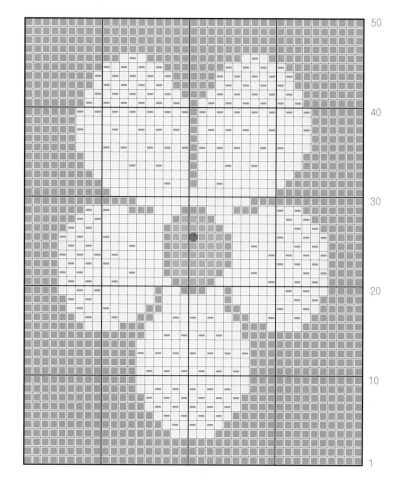

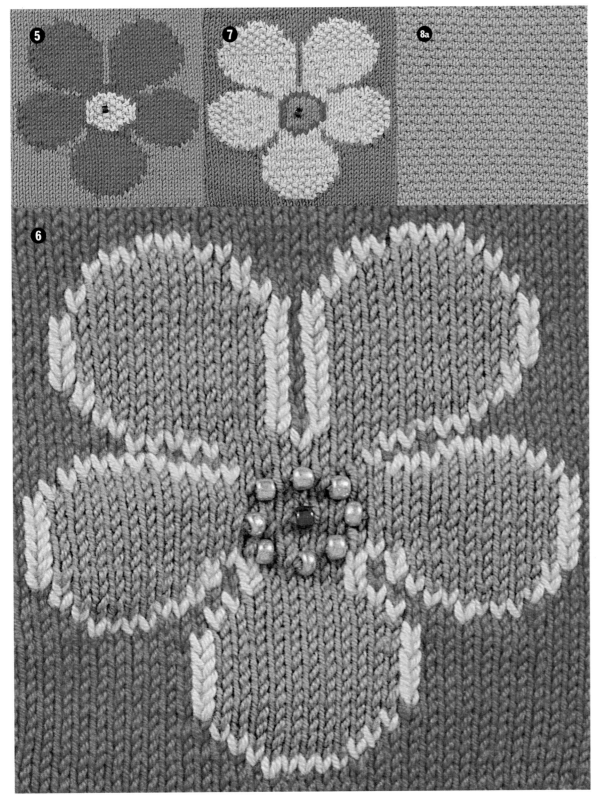

❽ Speckle

SIZE
6in × 6in (15cm × 15cm)

MATERIALS
1 pair US 5 (3.75mm/No. 9) needles

⁸ᵃ **First colorway** (×12 ◼)
Rowan Wool Cotton
1¾oz (50g) balls
    violet   ⅓

⁸ᵇ **Second colorway** (×12)
Rowan Wool Cotton
1¾oz (50g) balls
    pale yellow   ⅓

KNIT
Cast on 39 sts.
ROW 1 (RS): Knit.
ROW 2 (WS): (K1, P1) to last st, K1.
ROW 3 (RS): Knit.
ROW 4 (WS): K2 (P1, K1) to last st, K1.
ROW 5 (RS): Knit.
Rep rows 2-5, 11 times more.
(49 rows)
Bind (cast) off sts purlwise.

rock-a-bye-baby

I wanted to design a throw for a baby that moved away from the usual stereotypes associated with a project of this nature, so I decided to investigate the possibilities of playing with line and color in a geometric format. Being aware that color would influence the overall effect, I selected soft pastel shades to suggest a welcoming environment for a baby. Inspiration was also drawn from the multi-colored gummed paper shapes given to young children to play with at nursery groups. The addition of brightly colored outlines, which are embroidered onto circular shapes, and the fancy Lazy Daisy stitches add extra surface texture. A simple edging of garter stitch stripes completes this throw.

SIZE
38in x 38in (98cm x 98cm)

MATERIALS
1 pair US 2 (3.00mm/No. 11) needles
2 circular US 2 (2.75mm/No. 12)
    needles 39in (100cm) length

Yarn
Rowan Cotton Glace
1¾oz (50g) balls

mid blue	3
pink	3
soft yellow	5
deepest lilac	3
pale green	3
pale pink	3
bright yellow	3

Small amount of white

Quantities given for individual
squares are approximate fractions
of a ball.

GAUGE (TENSION)
25 sts and 34 rows to 4in (10cm)
measured over stockinette
(stocking) stitch using US 2
(3.00mm/No. 11) needles.

NOTE
Single stitch outlines on squares
⑨ and ⑪ can be Swiss-darned
after knitting (see page 123).

ABBREVIATIONS
See page 127.

FINISHING
The sizes given for the finished
afghan and individual squares
are approximate. The number of
stitches in a row, and the number
of rows in a square differ in some
instances. Therefore, when sewing
pieces together, ease the extra
stitches or extra rows into the
adjoining square.

Press the individual squares
using a damp cloth and warm iron.
Sew the squares together, joining
bound (cast) off edge of one
square to the cast on edge of the
next square, easing in stitches if
necessary, to form vertical strips.
Sew the vertical strips together,
easing in rows if necessary, to
create one block.

Edging

MATERIALS

2 circular 2.75mm (No. 12/US 2)
  needles 39in (100cm) length

Yarn

Rowan Cotton Glace
50g (1¾oz) balls
  soft yellow (A)   ⅘
  pale pink (B)   ⅓
  mid blue (C)   ⅓

KNIT

With RS facing and using A, pick
up and knit 259 sts along the
right-hand edge of the afghan.
Beg with a WS row cont to work in
garter stitch (knit every row), inc 1
st at each end of all RS rows, and
foll the color stripe sequence:
A, 5 rows; B, 2 rows; C, 2 rows.
Bind (cast) off sts knitwise.
Rep for left-hand edge of
the afghan.
With RS facing and using a
circular 2.75mm (No. 12/US 2)
needle and A, pick up and knit
252 sts along bottom edge of
the afghan.
Rep edging as for right-hand and
left-hand edges.
Rep for top edge of afghan.
Neatly sew border edges together.

Order of squares

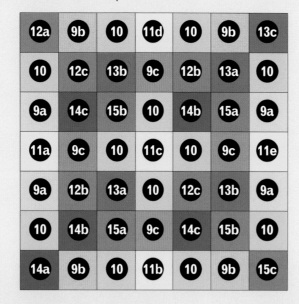

QUANTITY OF SQUARES

⑨ Ovals
  ⑨ₐ First colorway   4
  ⑨ᵦ Second colorway   4
  ⑨ᵪ Third colorway   4
⑩ Sweet stripes   12
⑪ Serenity
  ⑪ₐ First colorway   1
  ⑪ᵦ Second colorway   1
  ⑪ᵪ Third colorway   1
  ⑪ᵨ Fourth colorway   1
  ⑪ₑ Fifth colorway   1
⑫ Geometry 1
  ⑫ₐ First colorway   1
  ⑫ᵦ Second colorway   2
  ⑫ᵪ Third colorway   2

⑬ Geometry 2
  ⑬ₐ First colorway   2
  ⑬ᵦ Second colorway   2
  ⑬ᵪ Third colorway   1
⑭ Geometry 3
  ⑭ₐ First colorway   1
  ⑭ᵦ Second colorway   2
  ⑭ᵪ Third colorway   2
⑮ Geometry 4
  ⑮ₐ First colorway   2
  ⑮ᵦ Second colorway   2
  ⑮ᵪ Third colorway   1

❾ Ovals

SIZE

5¾in × 5¾in (14.5cm × 14.5cm)

MATERIALS

1 pair US 2 (3.00mm/No. 11) needles

⑨ₐ First colorway (×4 ⊞ ▣)

Rowan Cotton Glace
1¾oz (50g) balls
  ☐ pale pink (A)   ⅙
  ☐ pink (B)   1/12
  ☐ bright yellow (C)   1/25
  ▨ mid blue (D)   1/50

☐ K on RS, P on WS

⑨ᵦ Second colorway (×4)

Rowan Cotton Glace
1¾oz (50g) balls
  pale pink (A)   ⅙
  mid blue (B)   1/12
  bright yellow (C)   1/25
  pink (D)   1/50

⑨ᵪ Third colorway (×4)

Rowan Cotton Glace
1¾oz (50g) balls
  soft yellow (A)   ⅙
  deepest lilac (B)   1/12
  pale green (C)   1/25
  pale pink (D)   1/50

KNIT

Cast on 38 sts and work until
chart row 51 completed.
Bind (cast) off sts.

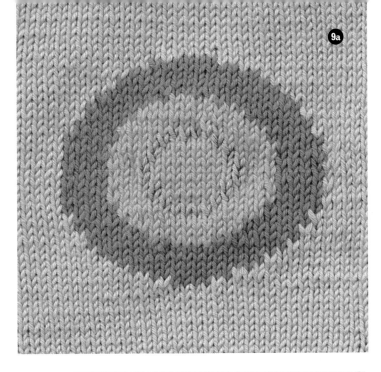

9a

⑩ Sweet stripes

SIZE
5¾in × 5¾in (14.5cm × 14.5cm)

MATERIALS
1 pair US 2 (3.00mm/No. 11) needles

Single colorway (×12 ▣)
Rowan Cotton Glace
1¾oz (50g) balls

pale green (A)	⅟10
pale pink (B)	⅟12
soft yellow (C)	⅟12
bright yellow (D)	⅟12

KNIT
Cast on 38 sts using A.
Working in stockinette (stocking) stitch continue in stripe patt rep as folls, beg with a RS row:
ROWS 1-3: **A**.

ROWS 4-7: **B**.
ROWS 8-11: **C**.
ROWS 12-15: **D**.
ROWS 16-19: **A**.
Rep rows 4-19 once more.
Rep rows 4-18 once more.
(50 rows)
Bind (cast) off sts.

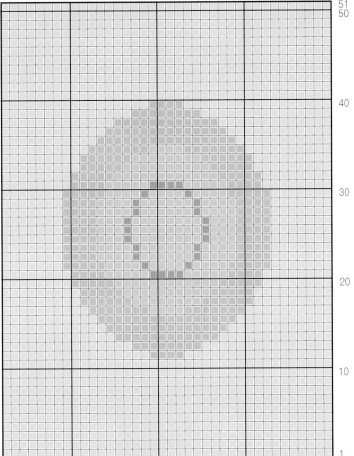

51
50

40

30

20

10

1

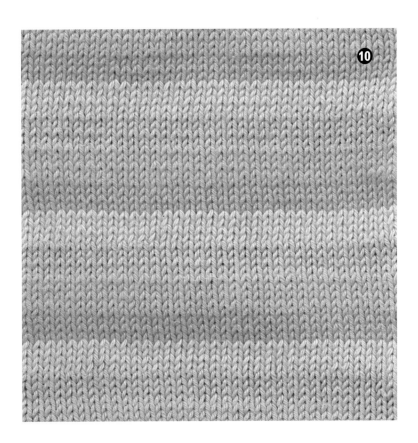

⑩

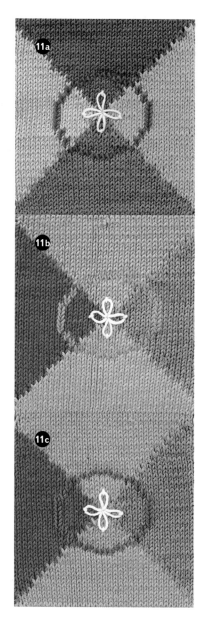

⓫ Serenity

SIZE
5¾in × 5¾in (14.5cm × 14.5cm)

MATERIALS
1 pair US 2 (3.00mm/No. 11) needles

⑪ₐ First colorway (×1 ▦ ▣)
Rowan Cotton Glace
1¾oz (50g) balls

◼ mid blue (A)	½
◻ pale green (B)	½
◻ soft yellow (C)	½
◼ deepest lilac (D)	½
◼ pink (E)	⅟₅₀

◎ Small amount of white
for Lazy Daisy stitch

☐ K on RS, P on WS

⑪ᵦ Second colorway (×1 ▣)
Rowan Cotton Glace
1¾oz (50g) balls

pale green (A)	½
mid blue (B)	½
pink (C)	½
pale pink (D)	½
bright yellow (E)	⅟₅₀

Small amount of white
for Lazy Daisy stitch

⑪꜀ Third colorway (×1 ▣)
Rowan Cotton Glace
1¾oz (50g) balls

bright yellow (A)	½
mid blue (B)	½
pink (C)	½
bright yellow (D)	½
deepest lilac (E)	⅟₅₀

Small amount of white
for Lazy Daisy stitch

⑪d Fourth colorway (×1)
Rowan Cotton Glace
1¾oz (50g) balls

pale pink (A)	½
pink (B)	½
mid blue (C)	½
pale green (D)	½
bright yellow (E)	⅟₅₀

Small amount of white
for Lazy Daisy stitch

⑪ₑ Fifth colorway (×1)
Rowan Cotton Glace
1¾oz (50g) balls

mid blue (A)	½
soft yellow (B)	½
pale green (C)	½
deepest lilac (D)	½
pink (E)	⅟₅₀

Small amount of white
for Lazy Daisy stitch

KNIT
Cast on 38 sts and work until
chart row 50 completed.
Bind (cast) off sts.
Using white, stitch Lazy Daisy onto
center of square after knitting (see
page 124).

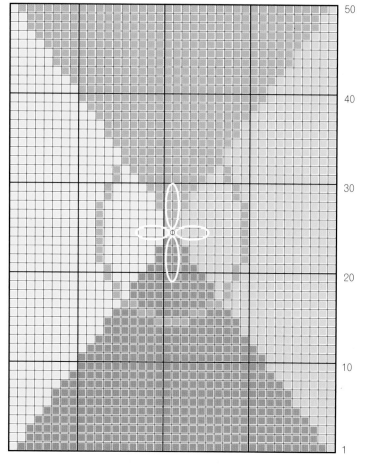

OPPOSITE: *The squares charted on
the following four pages have
diagonal lines that meet to form
diamond patterns when the
squares are sewn together.*

⑫ Geometry 1

SIZE
5¾in × 5¾in (14.5cm × 14.5cm)

MATERIALS
1 pair US 2 (3.00mm/No. 11) needles

⑫ᵃ First colorway (×1 ▦)
Rowan Cotton Glace
1¾oz (50g) balls
- ■ mid blue (A) — ¹⁄₁₆
- □ soft yellow (B) — ¹⁄₂
- ■ pink (C) — ¹⁄₁₆
- ■ deepest lilac (D) — ¹⁄₆

□ K on RS, P on WS

⊟ P on RS, K on WS

⑫ᵇ Second colorway (×2 ▣)
Rowan Cotton Glace
1¾oz (50g) balls
- deepest lilac (A) — ¹⁄₁₆
- pale green (B) — ¹⁄₂
- pink (C) — ¹⁄₁₆
- mid blue (D) — ¹⁄₆

⑫ᶜ Third colorway (×2 ▣)
Rowan Cotton Glace
1¾oz (50g) balls
- pale green (A) — ¹⁄₁₆
- mid blue (B) — ¹⁄₂
- soft yellow (C) — ¹⁄₁₆
- pink (D) — ¹⁄₆

KNIT
Cast on 38 sts and work until
chart row 52 completed.
Bind (cast) off sts.

⑬ Geometry 2

SIZE

5¾in × 5¾in (14.5cm × 14.5cm)

MATERIALS

1 pair US 2 (3.00mm/No. 11) needles

⑬ₐ First colorway (×2 ⊞)

Rowan Cotton Glace
1¾oz (50g) balls

☐	pale green (A)	¹⁄₁₆
	deepest lilac (B)	¹⁄₁₂
☐	soft yellow (C)	¹⁄₁₆
	pink (D)	¹⁄₆

☐ K on RS, P on WS

⊟ P on RS, K on WS

⑬ᵦ Second colorway (×2 ◼)

Rowan Cotton Glace
1¾oz (50g) balls

pink (A)	¹⁄₁₆
soft yellow (B)	¹⁄₁₂
mid blue (C)	¹⁄₁₆
deepest lilac (D)	¹⁄₆

⑬꜀ Third colorway (×1 ◼)

Rowan Cotton Glace
1¾oz (50g) balls

mid blue (A)	¹⁄₁₆
soft yellow (B)	¹⁄₁₂
deepest lilac (C)	¹⁄₁₆
pink (D)	¹⁄₆

KNIT

Cast on 38 sts and work until chart row 52 completed. Bind (cast) off sts.

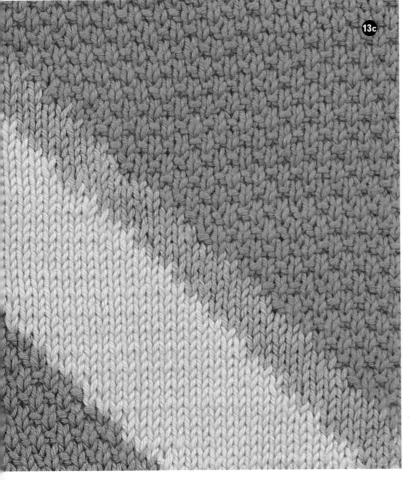

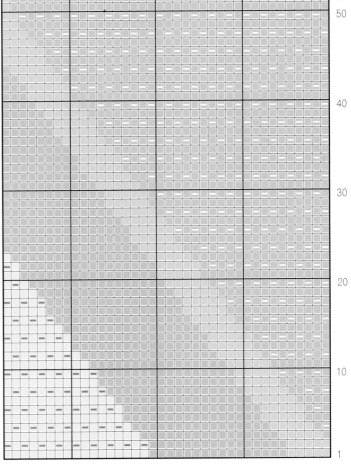

⓮ Geometry 3

SIZE

5¾in × 5¾in (14.5cm × 14.5cm)

MATERIALS

1 pair US 2 (3.00mm/No. 11) needles

14a First colorway (×1 ⊞)
Rowan Cotton Glace
1¾oz (50g) balls

■ mid blue (A)	1/16
■ pink (B)	1/6
□ soft yellow (C)	1/2
■ deepest lilac (D)	1/16

□ K on RS, P on WS

⊟ P on RS, K on WS

14b Second colorway (×2 ▣)
Rowan Cotton Glace
1¾oz (50g) balls

pale green (A)	1/16
pink (B)	1/6
deepest lilac (C)	1/2
soft yellow (D)	1/16

14c Third colorway (×2 ▣)
Rowan Cotton Glace
1¾oz (50g) balls

pink (A)	1/16
deepest lilac (B)	1/6
soft yellow (C)	1/2
mid blue (D)	1/16

KNIT

Cast on 38 sts and work until chart row 52 completed.
Bind (cast) off sts.

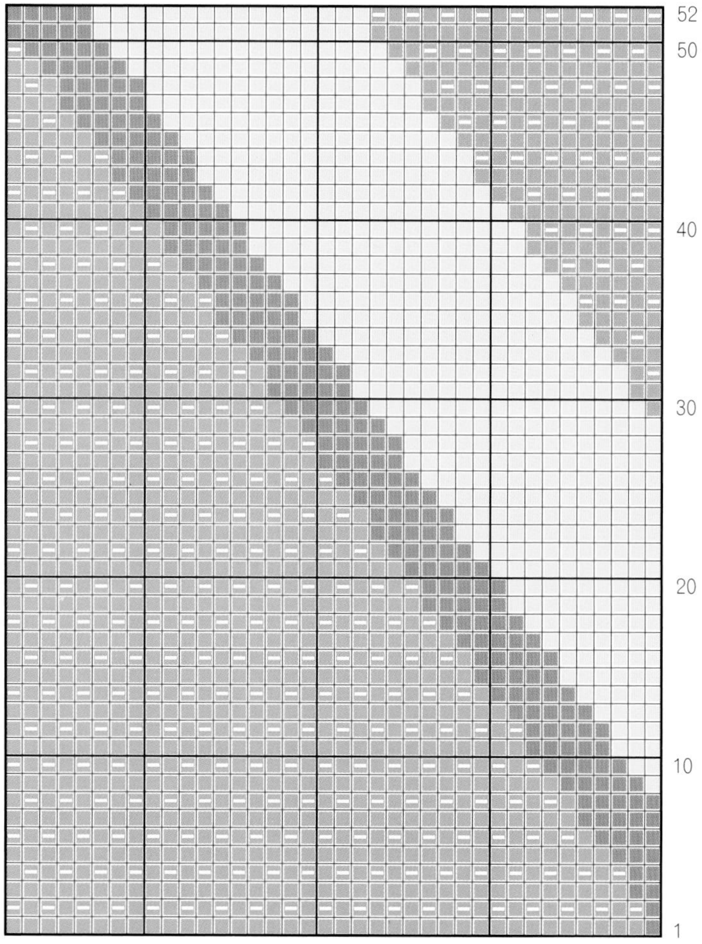

⓯ Geometry 4

SIZE
5¾in × 5¾in (14.5cm × 14.5cm)

MATERIALS
1 pair US 2 (3.00mm/No. 11) needles

⑮ₐ First colorway (×2 ⊞ ▣)
Rowan Cotton Glace
1¾oz (50g) balls
- ▨ mid blue (A) ⅛
- ▨ pink (B) ¹⁄₁₆
- ▨ pale green (C) ½
- ▨ deepest lilac (D) ¹⁄₁₆

☐ K on RS, P on WS

⊟ P on RS, K on WS

⑮ᵦ Second colorway (×2 ▣)
Rowan Cotton Glace
1¾oz (50g) balls
- pink (A) ⅛
- soft yellow (B) ¹⁄₁₆
- mid blue (C) ½
- pale green (D) ¹⁄₁₆

⑮ᵦ Third colorway (×1)
Rowan Cotton Glace
1¾oz (50g) balls
- deepest lilac (A) ⅛
- pink (B) ¹⁄₁₆
- soft yellow (C) ½
- mid blue (D) ¹⁄₁₆

KNIT
Cast on 38 sts and work until chart row 52 completed. Bind (cast) off sts.

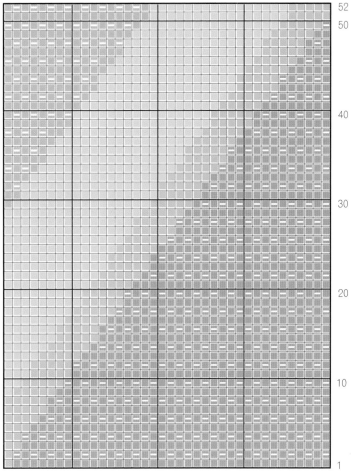

lithograph

In my student days I came in contact with various forms of printing and print-making. The centering and alignment of printing blocks is reflected in the geometric organization of this afghan. A reduced palette of black, cream and grays gives an air of of quiet restraint. The rich black of printer's ink led me to select a black yarn that contrasts well with tones of gray and cream. While the basic knitting for this afghan is relatively simple, the addition of Swiss-darning to almost every square gives a complex look. Circles, squares, zig-zags and horizontal lines are the dominant motifs, some embroidered onto the knitting and some created by a textured stitch. The reverse stockinette (stocking) stitch stripes in black and cream simulate lines of type. A simple edging seemed appropriate for this busy design.

SIZE
96in x 66in (243cm x 167cm)

MATERIALS
1 pair US 6 (4mm/No. 8) needles
2 circular US 3 (3.25mm/No. 10)
 needles 39in (100cm) length

Yarn
Rowan All Seasons Cotton
1¾oz (50g) balls
black	18
palest gray	16
deep blue-gray	12
cream	12

Rowan Magpie Aran
3½oz (100g) hanks
mid gray	5

Quantities given for individual
squares are approximate fractions
of a ball.

Beads
³⁄₁₆in (5mm) pebble beads
black	58
silver	58

Buttons
white ceramic buttons	18

GAUGE (TENSION)
19 sts and 27 rows to 4in (10cm)
measured over reverse stockinette
(stocking) stitch using US 6
(4mm/No. 8) needles.

NOTE
Single stitch outlines on squares
⑯ ⑰ ⑱ ⑲ ⑳ and ㉒ can be
Swiss-darned after knitting (see
page 123).

ABBREVIATIONS
See page 127.

FINISHING
The sizes given for the finished
afghan and individual squares are
approximate. The number of
stitches in a row, and the number
of rows in a square differ in some
instances. Therefore, when sewing
pieces together, ease the extra
stitches or extra rows into the
adjoining square.

Press the individual squares
using a damp cloth and warm iron.
Sew the squares together, joining
bound (cast) off edge of one
square to the cast on edge of the
next square, easing in stitches if
necessary, to form vertical strips.
Sew the vertical strips together,
easing in rows if necessary, to
create one block.

Edging

MATERIALS
2 circular US 3 (3.25mm/No. 10)
 needles 39in (100cm) length

Yarn
Rowan All Seasons Cotton
1¾oz (50g) balls
palest gray (A)	⅘
black (B)	½
cream (C)	⅗

KNIT
With RS facing and using A, pick
up and knit 481 sts along the right-
hand edge of the afghan.
Beg with a WS row, work as folls:
NEXT ROW (WS): A, knit.
NEXT ROW (RS): B, inc once into first
st, K to last 2 sts, inc once into
next st, K1.
Cast off sts knitwise using C.
Rep for left-hand edge of the afghan.
With RS facing and using A, pick up
and knit 337 sts along bottom edge
of the afghan.
Rep edging as for right-hand and
left-hand edges.
Rep for top edge of afghan.
Neatly sew border edges together.

Order of squares

16	18	21	17	16	18	21	17	16
18	20	17	19	18	20	17	19	18
21	17	22	18	21	17	22	18	21
17	19	18	20	17	19	18	20	17
16	18	21	17	16	18	21	17	16
18	20	17	19	18	20	17	19	18
21	17	22	18	21	17	22	18	21
17	19	18	20	17	19	18	20	17
16	18	21	17	16	18	21	17	16
18	20	17	19	18	20	17	19	18
21	17	22	18	21	17	22	18	21
17	19	18	20	17	19	18	20	17
16	18	21	17	16	18	21	17	16

QUANTITY OF SQUARES

⑯ Etched square	12
⑰ Imprint squares	29
⑱ Imprint circles	29
⑲ Imprint lines	12
⑳ Imprint zig-zags	12
㉑ Type	17
㉒ Etched circle	6

⑯ Etched square

SIZE
7½in × 7½in (19cm × 19cm)

MATERIALS
1 pair US 6 (4mm/No. 8) needles

Single colorway (×12 ⊞ ▣)
Rowan All Seasons Cotton
1¾oz (50g) balls

■	black	1/12
▢	palest gray	1/16
■	deep blue-gray	1/50

⊠ white ceramic buttons   1

▢ K on RS, P on WS

KNIT
Cast on 39 sts and work until chart row 49 completed.
Bind (cast) off sts.
Sew button onto center of square, as indicated on chart.

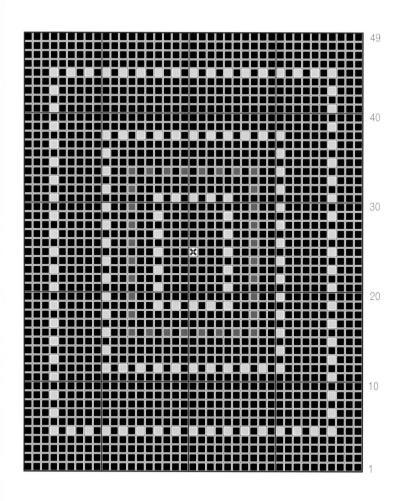

⓱ Imprint squares

SIZE

7½in × 7½in (19cm × 19cm)

MATERIALS

1 pair US 6 (4mm/No. 8) needles

Single colorway (×29 ⊞ ▣)
Rowan All Seasons Cotton
1¾oz (50g) balls
▦	palest gray	⅛
▦	deep blue-gray	⅛
▢	cream	⅛
■	black	¹⁄₅₀

Rowan Magpie Aran
3½oz (100g) hanks
▦	mid gray	¹⁄₁₆

³⁄₁₆in (5mm) pebble beads
●	black	1
⊙	silver	1

▢ K on RS, P on WS

⊟ P on RS, K on WS

KNIT

Cast on 40 sts and work until chart row 50 completed. Bind (cast) off sts.

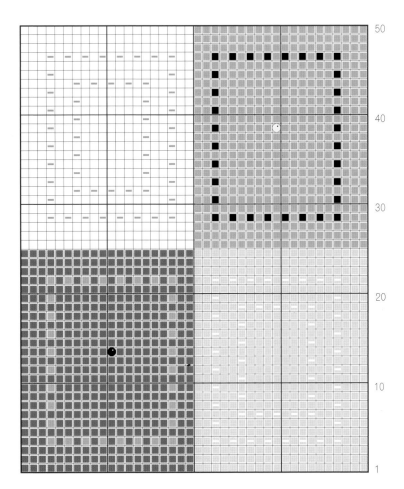

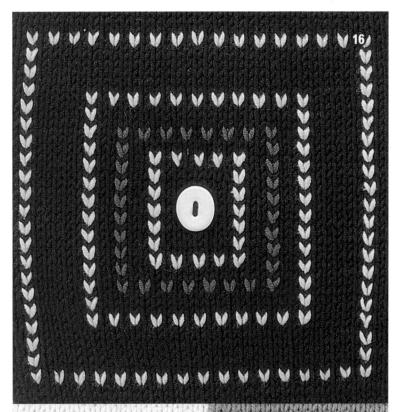

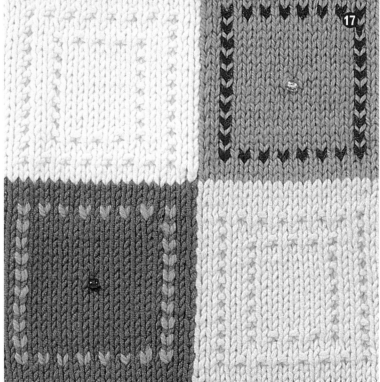

⑱ Imprint circles

SIZE
7½in × 7½in (19cm × 19cm)

MATERIALS
1 pair US 6 (4mm/No. 8) needles

Single colorway (×29 ⊞ ▣)
Rowan All Seasons Cotton
1¾oz (50g) balls

▢ palest gray	⅛
▓ deep blue-gray	⅛
■ black	1/50
▢ cream	⅛

Rowan Magpie Aran
3½oz (100g) hanks

▨ mid gray	1/16

³⁄₁₆in (5mm) pebble beads
● black	1
⊙ silver	1

▢ K on RS, P on WS

⊟ P on RS, K on WS

KNIT
Cast on 40 sts and work until chart row 50 completed. Bind (cast) off sts.

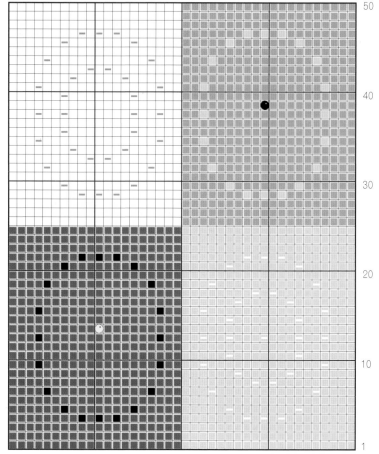

⓳ Imprint lines

☐ K on RS, P on WS

⊟ P on RS, K on WS

SIZE
7½in × 7½in (19cm × 19cm)

MATERIALS
1 pair US 6 (4mm/No. 8) needles

Single colorway (×12 ⊞ ▣)
Rowan All Seasons Cotton
1¾oz (50g) balls

▨ palest gray	⅛
▨ deep blue-gray	⅙
■ black	1/50
☐ cream	⅛

Rowan Magpie Aran
3½oz (100g) hanks
▨ mid gray	1/16

KNIT
Cast on 40 sts and work until chart row 50 completed. Bind (cast) off sts.

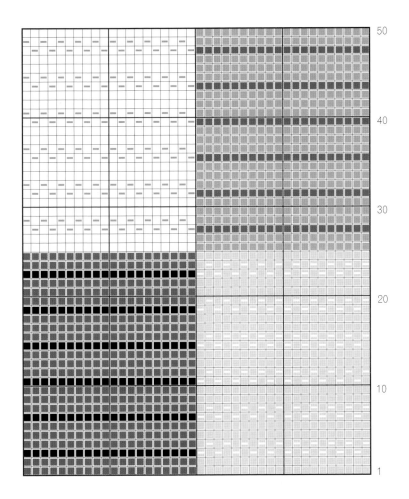

⓴ Imprint zig-zags

☐ K on RS, P on WS

⊟ P on RS, K on WS

SIZE
7½in × 7½in (19cm × 19cm)

MATERIALS
1 pair US 6 (4mm/No. 8) needles

Single colorway (×12 ⊞ ▣)
Rowan All Seasons Cotton
1¾oz (50g) balls

▨ palest gray	⅛
▨ deep blue-gray	⅛
☐ cream	⅛
■ black	1/50

Rowan Magpie Aran
3½oz (100g) hanks
▨ mid gray	1/16

KNIT
Cast on 40 sts and work until chart row 50 completed. Bind (cast) off sts.

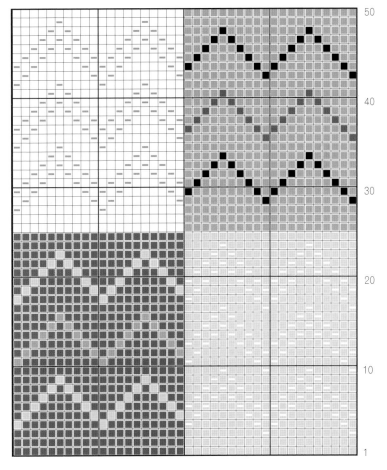

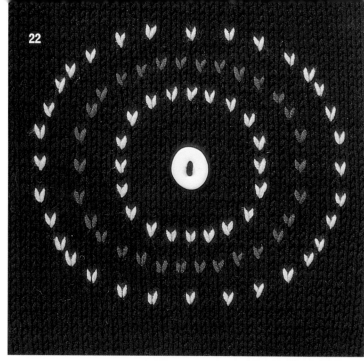

㉑ Type

SIZE
7½in × 7½in (19cm × 19cm)

MATERIALS
1 pair US 6 (4mm/No. 8) needles

Single colorway (×17 ▣)
Rowan All Seasons Cotton
1¾oz (50g) balls
    black (A)   ⅓
    palest gray (B)   ⅙

KNIT
Cast on 39 sts using A.
ROW 1 (RS): A, purl.
ROW 2 (WS): A, knit.
ROW 3 (RS): As row 1.
ROW 4 (WS): B, knit.
ROW 5 (RS): B, purl.
ROW 6 (WS): As row 2.
ROW 7 (RS): As row 1.
ROW 8 (WS): As row 2.
ROW 9 (RS): As row 1.
Rep rows 4–9, 6 times more.
Rep rows 4–8 once more.
(50 rows)
Bind (cast) off sts.

㉒ Etched circle

SIZE
7½in × 7½in (19cm × 19cm)

MATERIALS
1 pair US 6 (4mm/No. 8) needles

Single colorway (×6 ▦ ▣)
Rowan All Seasons Cotton
1¾oz (50g) balls
■ black   ½
▢ palest gray   1/25
▦ deep blue-gray   1/50

☒ white ceramic buttons   1

☐ K on RS, P on WS

KNIT
Cast on 39 sts and work until
chart row 50 completed.
Bind (cast) off sts.

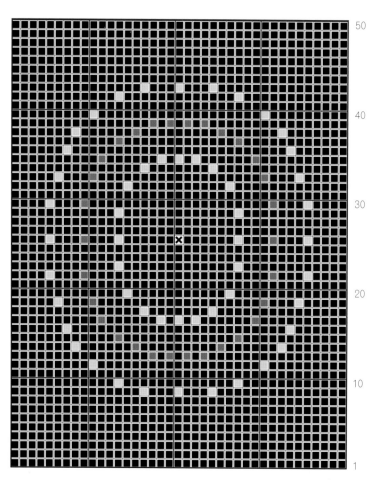

OPPOSITE: *The graphic patterns on these squares combine to produce a clean, contemporary look.*

candy mixture

Our village sweet shop was always an enticing place to stop off at on the way back from school. Rows of glass jars containing much-loved traditional confectionery filled the higher shelves, while within easier reach were cartons of goodies for us to spend our pocket-money on. Many of the old favorites are still enjoyed by today's schoolchildren. These candy-colored sweets were the source of inspiration for this afghan. Squares and circles are the dominant shapes, combined with sugary stripes, and to suggest sweet wrappers I introduced small amounts of lurex to the knitting to capture the crinkly effects of cellophane and foil. Brilliant white beads are used sporadically to represent scatterings of icing sugar. This was truly an edible inspiration!

SIZE
66in x 66in (168cm x 168cm)

MATERIALS
1 pair US 6 (4mm/No. 8) needles
2 circular US 3 (3.25mm/No. 10)
   needles 39in (100cm) length
Cable needle

Yarn
Rowan All Seasons Cotton
1¾oz (50g) balls

purple	6
white	2
light turquoise	11
pale yellow	12
chocolate brown	1
red	12

Rowan Summer Tweed
1¾oz (50g) hanks

orange	1

Rowan Lurex Shimmer
1oz (25g) balls

turquoise	3
(used triple throughout)	
shiny pink	4
(knitted together with	
pale pink throughout)	

Rowan Cotton Glace
1¾oz (50g) balls

pale pink	3
(knitted together with	
shiny pink throughout)	

Quantities given for individual squares are approximate fractions of a ball.

Beads
³⁄₁₆in (5mm) pebble beads

white	480
yellow	312

GAUGE (TENSION)
19 sts and 27 rows to 4in (10cm) measured over stockinette (stocking) stitch using US 6 (4mm/No. 8) needles.

NOTE
Single stitch outlines on squares ㉓ and ㉛ can be Swiss-darned after knitting (see page 123).

ABBREVIATIONS
See page 127.

FINISHING
The sizes given for the finished afghan and individual squares are approximate. The number of stitches in a row, and the number of rows in a square differ in some instances. Therefore, when sewing pieces together, ease the extra stitches or extra rows into the adjoining square.

Press the individual squares using a damp cloth and warm iron. Sew the squares together, joining bound (cast) off edge of one square to the cast on edge of the next square, easing in stitches if necessary, to form vertical strips. Sew the vertical strips together, easing in rows if necessary, to create one block.

Edging

MATERIALS
2 circular US 3 (3.25mm/No. 10) needles 39in (100cm) length

Yarn
Rowan All Seasons Cotton
1¾oz (50g) balls

red	1½

KNIT
With RS facing, pick up and knit 333 sts along the right-hand edge of the afghan.
Beg with a WS row, work 8 rows in garter stitch (knit every row), inc 1 st at each end of all RS rows.
Cast off sts knitwise.
Rep for left-hand edge of the afghan.
With RS facing, pick up and knit 327 sts along bottom edge of the afghan.
Rep edging as for right-hand and left-hand edges.
Rep for top edge of afghan.
Neatly sew border edges together.

Order of squares

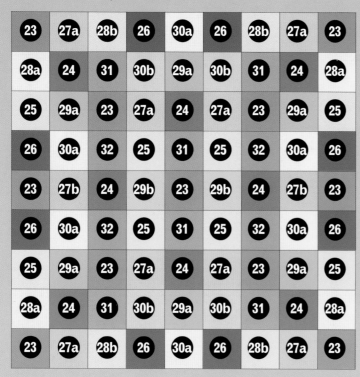

QUANTITY OF SQUARES

㉓	Candy squares	11
㉔	Icing sugar	8
㉕	Jelly beans	8
㉖	Strawberry stripe	8
㉗	Sweetie wrapper	
㉗ₐ	First colorway	8
㉗ᵦ	Second colorway	2
㉘	Textured circles	
㉘ₐ	First colorway	4
㉘ᵦ	Second colorway	4
㉙	Sherbet	
㉙ₐ	First colorway	6
㉙ᵦ	Second colorway	2
㉚	Textured squares	
㉚ₐ	First colorway	4
㉚ᵦ	Second colorway	4
㉛	Candy mixture	6
㉜	Rock candy	4

㉓ Candy squares

SIZE
7in × 7in (18cm × 18cm)

MATERIALS
1 pair US 6 (4mm/No. 8) needles

Single colorway (×11 ⊞ ▣)
Rowan All Seasons Cotton
1¾oz (50g) balls

▪	purple	⅕
☐	white	⅛
▪	light turquoise	⅙
☐	pale yellow	¹⁄₅₀

Rowan Summer Tweed
1¾oz (50g) hanks

▪	orange	¹⁄₅₀

☐ K on RS, P on WS

⊟ P on RS, K on WS

KNIT
Cast on 39 sts and work until chart row 50 completed.
Bind (cast) off sts.

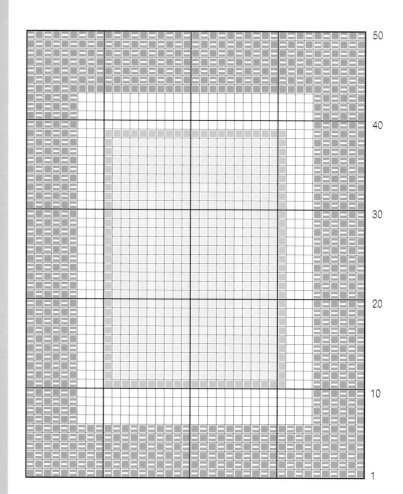

㉔ Icing sugar

SIZE

7in × 7in (18cm × 18cm)

MATERIALS

1 pair US 6 (4mm/No. 8) needles

Single colorway (×8 ⊞ ◼)

Rowan All Seasons Cotton
1¾oz (50g) balls

◼ red   ½

³⁄₁₆in (5mm) pebble beads
◌ white   48

☐ K on RS, P on WS

KNIT

Thread on 48 beads.
Cast on 40 sts and work until
chart row 50 completed.
Bind (cast) off sts.

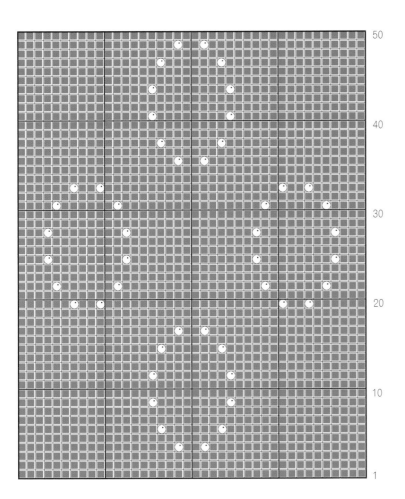

㉕ Jelly beans

SIZE
7in × 7in (18cm × 18cm)

MATERIALS
1 pair US 6 (4mm/No. 8) needles

Single colorway (×8 ⊞ ▣)
Rowan All Seasons Cotton
1¾oz (50g) balls

⬜ light turquoise	⅓
⬛ purple	¹⁄₂₅
⬜ pale yellow	¹⁄₂₅
⬛ chocolate brown	¹⁄₂₅

Rowan Summer Tweed
1¾oz (50g) hanks
⬜ orange   ¹⁄₂₅

Rowan Lurex Shimmer
1oz (25g) balls
⬜ shiny pink   ¹⁄₂₅
(knitted together with
pale pink throughout)

Rowan Cotton Glace
1¾oz (50g) balls
⬜ pale pink   ¹⁄₅₀
(knitted together with
shiny pink throughout)

☐ K on RS, P on WS

KNIT
Cast on 40 sts and work until
chart row 50 completed.
Bind (cast) off sts.

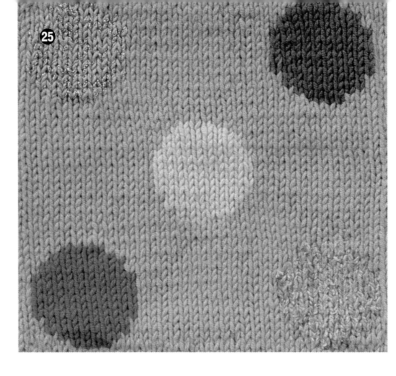

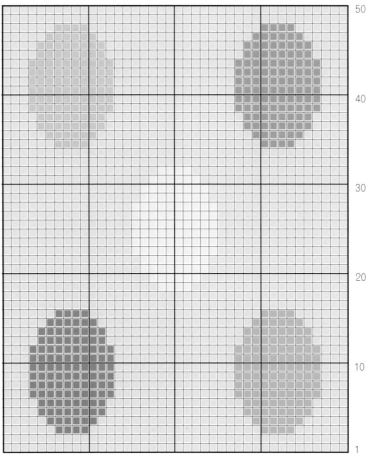

㉖ Strawberry stripe

SIZE
7in × 7in (18cm × 18cm)

MATERIALS
1 pair US 6 (4mm/No. 8) needles

Single colorway (×8 ▣)
Rowan All Seasons Cotton
1¾oz (50g) balls

red (A)	⅕
purple (B)	⅓

³⁄₁₆in (5mm) pebble beads
yellow   39

KNIT
Thread 39 beads onto B.
Cast on 37 sts using A.
ROW 1 (RS): A, knit.
ROW 2 (WS): A, purl.
ROW 3 (RS): B, knit.
ROW 4 (WS): B, purl.
ROW 5 (RS): B, K3, (pb, K5)
5 times, pb, K3.
ROW 6 (WS): B, purl.
ROW 7 (RS): As row 1.
ROW 8 (WS): As row 2.
ROW 9 (RS): As row 1.
ROW 10 (WS): As row 4.
ROW 11 (RS): As row 3.
ROW 12 (WS): B, P6, (pb, P5)
5 times, P1.
ROW 13 (RS): As row 3.
ROW 14 (WS): As row 2.
ROW 15 (RS): As row 1.
ROW 16 (WS): As row 2.
Rep rows 3-16 twice more.
Rep rows 3-8 once more.
(50 rows)
Bind (cast) off sts.

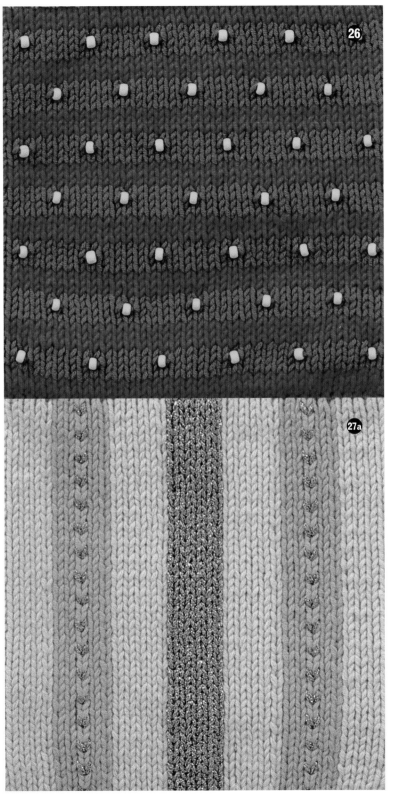

㉗ Sweetie wrapper

SIZE

7in × 7in (18cm × 18cm)

MATERIALS

1 pair US 6 (4mm/No. 8) needles

㉗ᵃ First colorway (×8 ◼)

Rowan All Seasons Cotton
1¾oz (50g) balls
    pale yellow (A)   ⅓
    light turquoise (B)   ⅙

Rowan Lurex Shimmer
1oz (25g) balls
    turquoise (C)   ⅙
    (used triple throughout)

㉗ᵇ Second colorway (×2 ◼)

Rowan All Seasons Cotton
1¾oz (50g) balls
    light turquoise (B)   ⅙

Rowan Lurex Shimmer
1oz (25g) balls
    turquoise (C)   ⅙
    (used triple throughout)
    shiny pink (A)   ⅕
    (knitted together with
    pale pink throughout)

Rowan Cotton Glace
1¾oz (50g) balls
    pale pink (A)   ⅕
    (knitted together with
    shiny pink throughout)

KNIT

Cast on 37 sts using A.

ROW 1 (RS): K6A, K5B, K5A, K5C, K5A, K5B, K6A.

ROW 2 (WS): P6A, P5B, P5A, P5C, P5A, P5B, P6A.

ROW 3 (RS): K6A, K2B, K1C, K2B, K5A, K5C, K5A, K2B, K1C, K2B, K6A.

ROW 4 (WS): As row 2.

ROW 5 (RS): As row 1.

ROW 6 (WS): P6A, P2B, P1C, P2B, P5A, P5C, P5A, P2B, P1C, P2B, P6A.

Rep these 6 rows, 7 times more.
Rep rows 1-2 once more.
(50 rows)
Bind (cast) off sts.

㉘ Textured circles

SIZE

7in × 7in (18cm × 18cm)

MATERIALS

1 pair US 6 (4mm/No. 8) needles

㉘ᵃ First colorway (×4 ■)

Rowan All Seasons Cotton
1¾oz (50g) balls
    pale yellow   ½

㉘ᵇ Second colorway (×4)

Rowan All Seasons Cotton
1¾oz (50g) balls
    light turquoise   ½

KNIT

Cast on 38 sts.

ROW 1 (RS): Purl.
ROW 2 (WS): Knit.
ROW 3 (RS): P5, (K4, P8) twice, K4, P5.
ROW 4 (WS): K4, (P6, K6) twice, P6, K4.
ROW 5 (RS): P3, (K8, P4) twice, K8, P3.
ROW 6 (WS): K3, (P8, K4) twice, P8, K3.
ROW 7 (RS): P2, (K10, P2) 3 times.
ROW 8 (WS): K2, (P4, K2) 6 times.
ROW 9 (RS): P2, (K3, P4, K3, P2) 3 times.
ROW 10 (WS): K2, (P3, K4, P3, K2) 3 times.
ROW 11 (RS): P2, (K4, P2) 6 times.
ROW 12 (WS): K2, (P10, K2) 3 times.
ROW 13 (RS): As row 5.
ROW 14 (WS): As row 6.
ROW 15 (RS): P4, (K6, P6) twice, K6, P4.
ROW 16 (WS): K5, (P4, K8) twice, P4, K5.
Rep rows 1-16 twice more.
Rep rows 1-2 once more.
(50 rows)
Bind (cast) off sts.

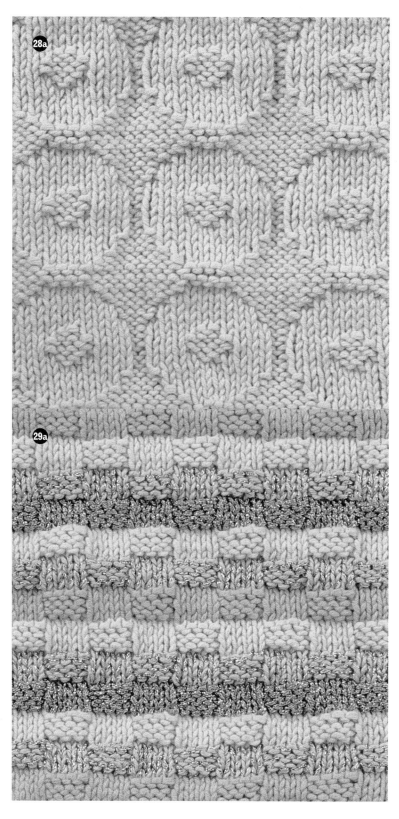

㉙ Sherbet

SIZE

18cm × 18cm (7in × 7in)

MATERIALS

1 pair 4mm (No. 8/US 6) needles

㉙ᵃ First colorway (×6 ⊞ ■)

Rowan All Seasons Cotton
1¾oz (50g) balls
☐ light turquoise (A)   ⅛
☐ pale yellow (C)   ⅙

Rowan Lurex Shimmer
1oz (25g) balls
☐ turquoise (D)   ⅕
    (used triple throughout)
☐ shiny pink (B)   ⅙
    (knitted together with
    pale pink throughout)

Rowan Cotton Glace
1¾oz (50g) balls
☐ pale pink (B)   ⅛
    (knitted together with
    shiny pink throughout)

☐ K on RS, P on WS

⊟ P on RS, K on WS

29b Second colorway (×2 ▣)

Rowan All Seasons Cotton
1¾oz (50g) balls

pale yellow (B)	⅙
light turquoise (C)	⅙
red (D)	⅒

Rowan Lurex Shimmer
1oz (25g) balls

shiny pink (A) (knitted together with pale pink throughout)	⅛

Rowan Cotton Glace
1¾oz (50g) balls

pale pink (A) (knitted together with shiny pink throughout)	1/12

KNIT

Cast on 38 sts and work until chart row 52 completed.
Bind (cast) off sts.

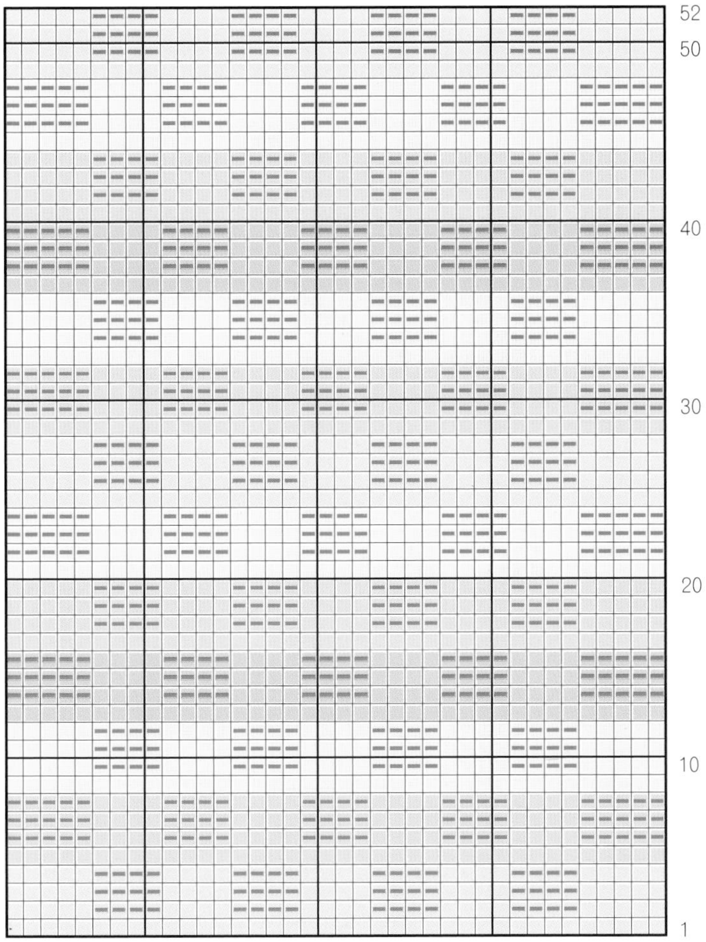

30 Textured squares

SIZE

7in × 7in (18cm × 18cm)

MATERIALS

1 pair US 6 (4mm/No. 8) needles

30a First colorway (×4 ⊞ ▣)

Rowan All Seasons Cotton
1¾oz (50g) balls

☐ pale yellow	½

☐ K on RS, P on WS

⊟ P on RS, K on WS

30b Second colorway (×4)

Rowan Lurex Shimmer
1oz (25g) balls

shiny pink (knitted together with pale pink throughout)	½

Rowan Cotton Glace
1¾oz (50g) balls

pale pink (knitted together with shiny pink throughout)	⅓

KNIT

Cast on 39 sts and work until chart row 54 completed.
Bind (cast) off sts.

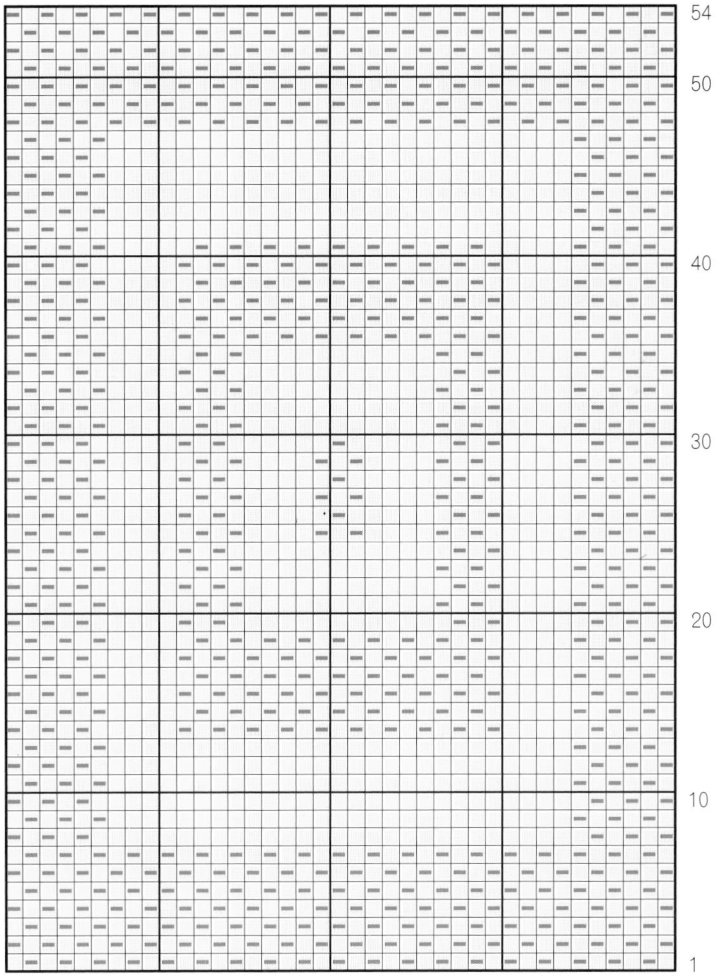

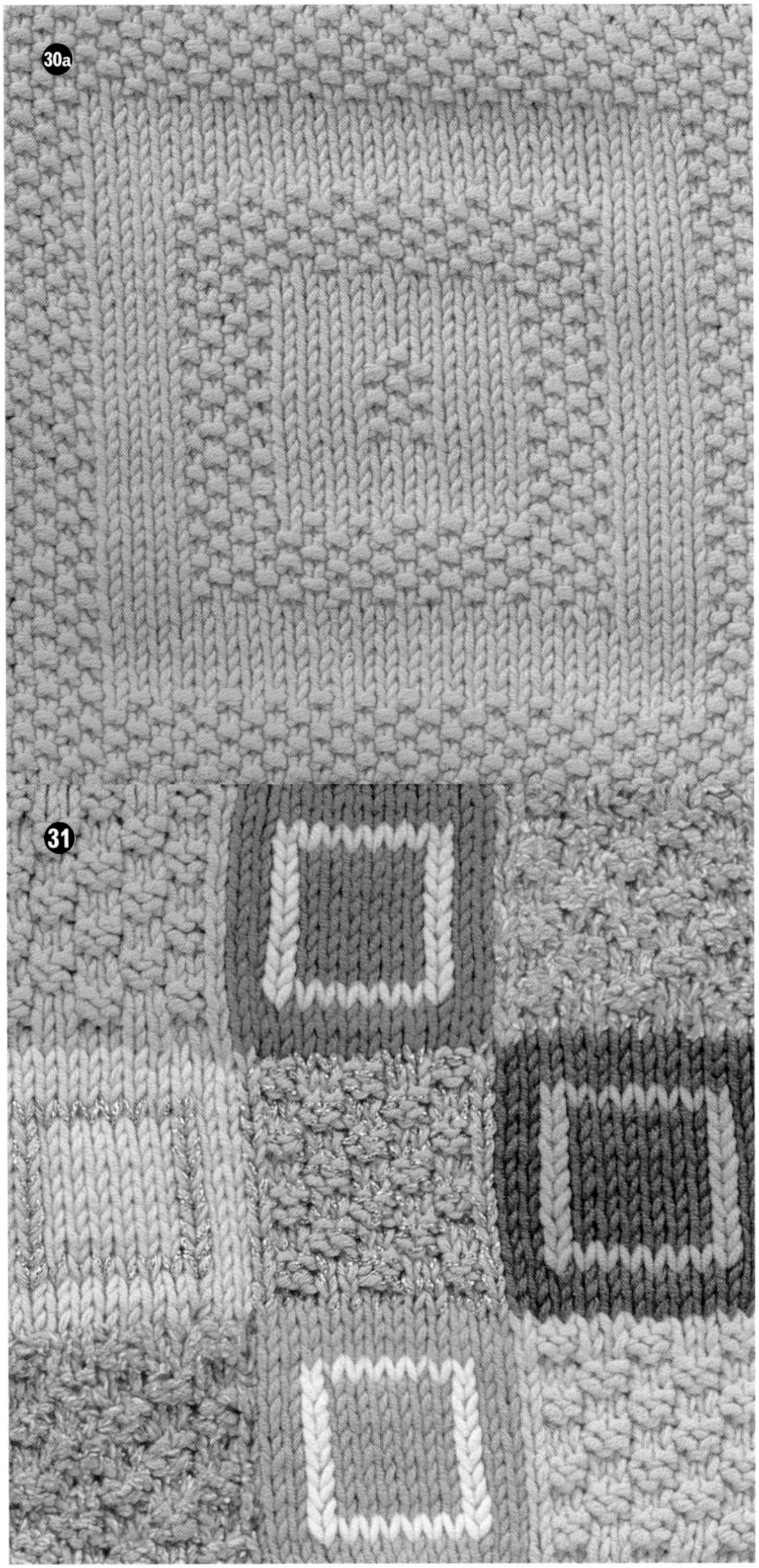

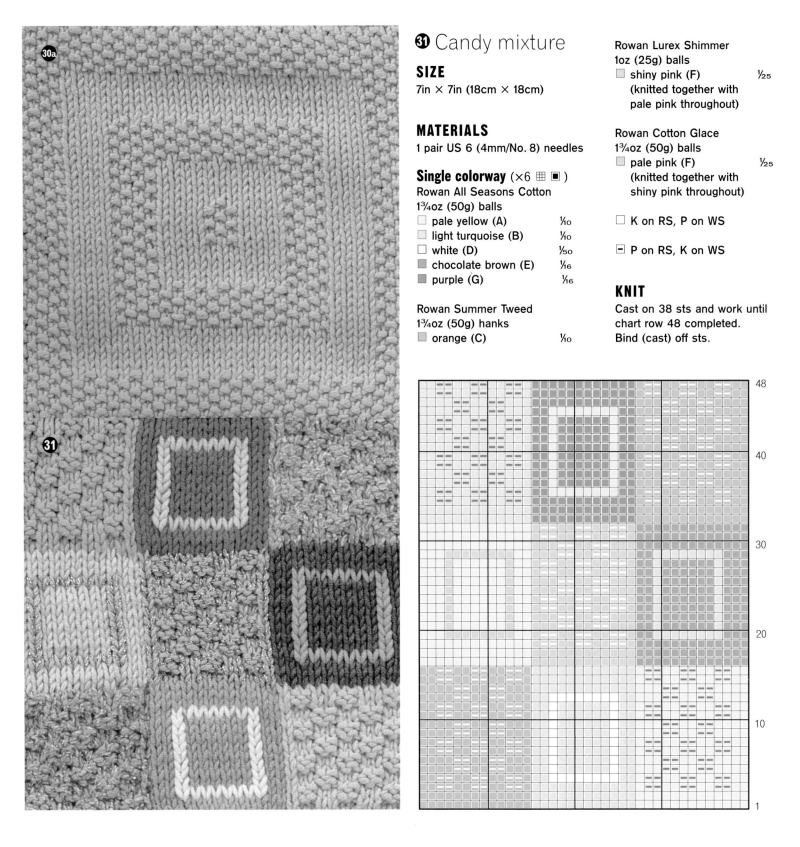

❸❶ Candy mixture

SIZE
7in × 7in (18cm × 18cm)

MATERIALS
1 pair US 6 (4mm/No. 8) needles

Single colorway (×6 ▦ ▣)
Rowan All Seasons Cotton
1¾oz (50g) balls
- pale yellow (A) 1/10
- light turquoise (B) 1/10
- white (D) 1/50
- chocolate brown (E) 1/16
- purple (G) 1/16

Rowan Summer Tweed
1¾oz (50g) hanks
- orange (C) 1/10

Rowan Lurex Shimmer
1oz (25g) balls
- shiny pink (F) 1/25
  (knitted together with pale pink throughout)

Rowan Cotton Glace
1¾oz (50g) balls
- pale pink (F) 1/25
  (knitted together with shiny pink throughout)

- K on RS, P on WS

- ⊟ P on RS, K on WS

KNIT
Cast on 38 sts and work until chart row 48 completed.
Bind (cast) off sts.

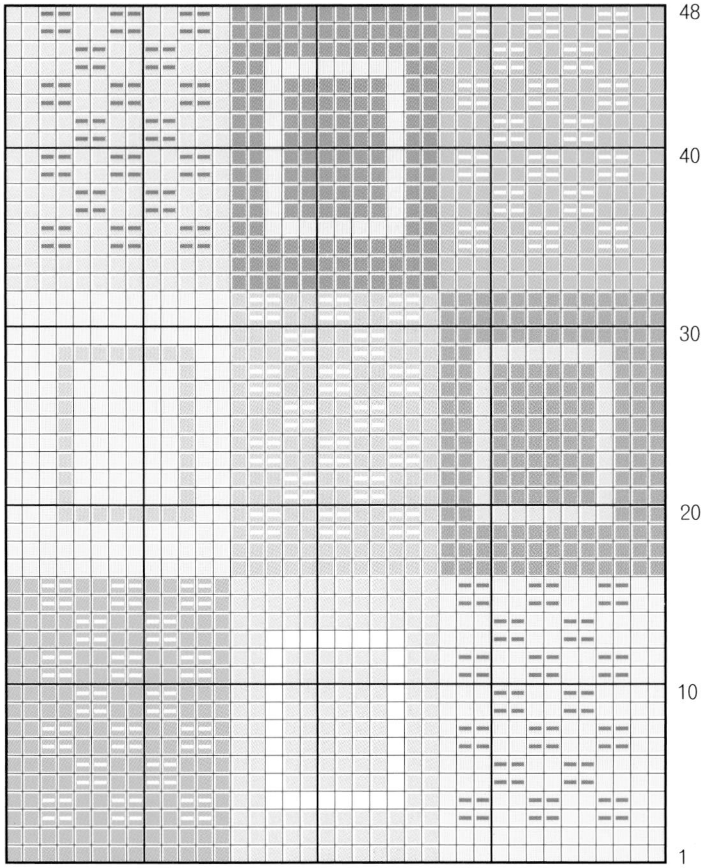

🄷 Rock candy

SIZE
7in × 7in (18cm × 18cm)

MATERIALS
1 pair US 6 (4mm/No. 8) needles
1 cable needle

Single colorway (×4 ▦ ◼)
Rowan All Seasons Cotton
1¾oz (50g) balls

◼ purple (A)		⅓
☐ pale yellow (B)		⅙
☐ light turquoise (D)		1⁄12

Rowan Lurex Shimmer
1oz (25g) balls

☐ shiny pink (C)		¼
(knitted together with		
pale pink throughout)		

Rowan Cotton Glace
1¾oz (50g) balls

☐ pale pink (C)		⅙
(knitted together with		
shiny pink throughout)		

³⁄₁₆in (5mm) pebble beads
⊙ white   24

☐ K on RS, P on WS

▭ P on RS, K on WS

▱▱▱ c6b

KNIT
Thread 16 beads onto B and
8 beads onto D.
Cast on 37 sts using A.
ROW 1 (RS) (INC): **P2A, incA** once
into next 3 sts, **P1A, K2B, P1B,
K2B, P1C, incC** once into next
3 sts, **P1C, K2D, P1D, K2D, P1A,
incA** once into next 3 sts, **P1A,
K2B, P1B, K2B, P1C, incC** once
into next 3 sts, **P2C.** *(49 sts)*
ROW 2 (WS): **K2C, P6C, K1C, P2B,
K1B, P2B, K1A, P6A, K1A, P2D,
K1D, P2D, K1C, P6C, K1C, P2B,
K1B, P2B, K1A, P6A, K2A.**
Beg with a RS row cont to
work from chart until chart row
49 completed.
NEXT ROW (WS) (DEC): **K2C, P2togC**
3 times, **K1C, P2B, K1B, P2B, K1A,**
P2togA 3 times, **K1A, P2D, K1D,
P2D, K1C, P2togC** 3 times, **K1C,
P2B, K1B, P2B, K1A, P2togA**
3 times, **K2A.** *(37 sts)*
Bind (cast) off sts.

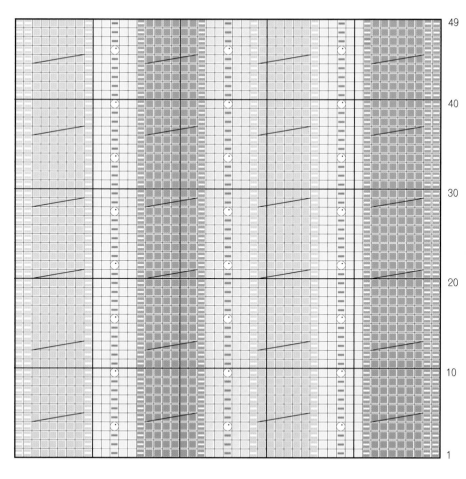

mosaic

Whenever I travel abroad I am always excited about the prospect of finding new ideas for my design work. When I spent some time in Portugal a few years ago, I discovered the traditional "Aluzejo" – the decorative, glazed wall tiles that are found everywhere in Portugal. Wandering around hot and dusty street markets I was lucky enough to unearth some beautiful old tiles, which were hidden away under piles of bric-a-brac. The glazes and textures on these ceramics have been a source of inspiration for me, and I have explored the geometric repeating patterns that can be achieved by juxtaposing the individual tiles. I was excited by the way in which unexpected results would emerge when I moved the tiles around, imitating the action of a kaleidoscope. To my delight I found that these geometric formations could be changed by simply moving and rotating the separate tiles. This is a feature that I have experimented with in Mosaic, which is created from just three basic squares.

SIZE
75in x 52in (190cm x 132cm)

MATERIALS
1 pair US 5 (3.75mm/No. 9) needles
2 circular US 3 (3.25mm/No. 10) needles 39in (100cm) length

Yarn
Rowan Wool Cotton
1¾oz (50g) balls

pale yellow	5
green	6
violet	4
rose pink	6
magenta	5
mid blue	5

Rowan Rowanspun DK
1¾oz (50g) hanks

purple tweed	3
green tweed	1
blue tweed	3
orange tweed	1

Quantities given for individual squares are approximate fractions of a ball.

GAUGE (TENSION)
24 sts and 32 rows to 4in (10cm) measured over patterned stockinette (stocking) stitch using US 5 (3.75mm/No. 9) needles.

NOTE
Single stitch outline on square ㉟ can be Swiss-darned after knitting (see page 123).

ABBREVIATIONS
See page 127.

FINISHING
The sizes given for the finished afghan and individual squares are approximate. The number of stitches in a row, and the number of rows in a square differ in some instances. Therefore, when sewing pieces together, ease the extra stitches or extra rows into the adjoining square.

Press the individual squares using a damp cloth and warm iron. Sew the squares together, joining bound (cast) off edge of one square to the cast on edge of the next square, easing in stitches if necessary, to form vertical strips. Sew the vertical strips together, easing in rows if necessary, to create one block.

Edging

MATERIALS

2 circular US 3 (3.25mm/No. 10)
needles 39in (100cm) length

Yarn

Rowan Wool Cotton
1¾oz (50g) balls
    magenta (A)   1⅘
    mid blue (B)   ½

KNIT

With RS facing and using A, pick
up and knit 468 sts along the
right-hand edge of the afghan.
Beg with a WS row cont to work in
garter st (knit every row), inc 1 st
at each end of all RS rows, until
6 rows are completed.
Cast off sts knitwise using B.
Rep for left-hand edge of
the afghan.
With RS facing and using A, pick
up and knit 324 sts along bottom
edge of the afghan.
Rep edging as for right-hand and
left-hand edges.
Rep for top edge of afghan.
Neatly sew border edges together.

Order of squares

QUANTITY OF SQUARES

㉝ Quattro	6
㉞ Nonetto	
㉞ₐ First colorway	28
㉞ᵦ Second colorway	24
㉟ Ravenna	
㉟ₐ First colorway	31
㉟ᵦ Second colorway	28

㉝ Quattro

SIZE

6in × 6in (15cm × 15cm)

MATERIALS

1 pair US 5 (3.75mm/No. 9) needles

Single colorway (×6 ▣)

Rowan Wool Cotton
1¾oz (50g) balls
    rose pink (A)   ⅛
    violet (B)   ⅛

KNIT

Cast on 38 sts using A.
ROW 1 (RS): K19A, K19B.
ROW 2 (WS): P19B, P19A.
Rep these 2 rows, 11 times more.
Rep row 1 once more.
NEXT ROW (WS): P19A, P19B.
NEXT ROW (RS): K19B, K19A.
Rep the last 2 rows, 11 times more.
NEXT ROW (WS): P19A, P19B.
(50 rows)
Bind (cast) off sts.

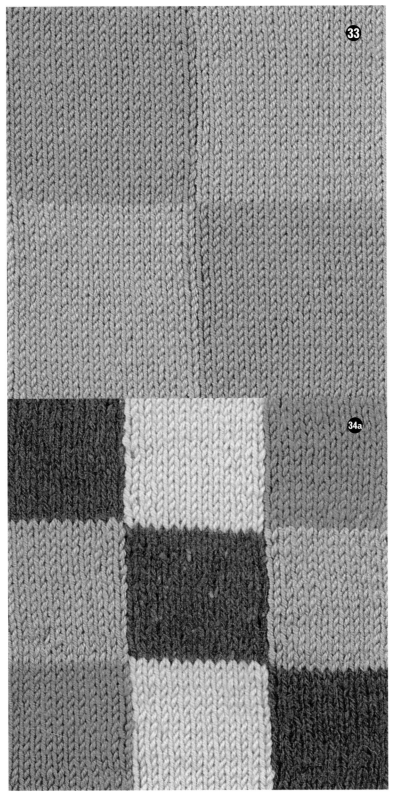

 Nonetto

SIZE

6in × 6in (15cm × 15cm)

MATERIALS

1 pair US 5 (3.75mm/No. 9) needles

First colorway (×28 ■)

Rowan Wool Cotton
1¾oz (50g) balls
    pale yellow (B)   ¹⁄₁₆
    green (C)   ¹⁄₁₆
    violet (D)   ¹⁄₁₆

Rowan Rowanspun DK
1¾oz (50g) balls
    purple tweed (A)   ¹⁄₁₆
    green tweed (E)   ¹⁄₂₅

Second colorway (×24 ■)

Rowan Wool Cotton
1¾oz (50g) hanks
    rose pink (A)   ¹⁄₁₆
    magenta (B)   ¹⁄₁₆
    mid blue (C)   ¹⁄₁₆

Rowan Rowanspun DK
1¾oz (50g) hanks
    blue tweed (D)   ¹⁄₁₆
    orange tweed (E)   ¹⁄₂₅

KNIT

Cast on 38sts using A.
ROW 1 (RS): **K13A, K12B, K13C.**
ROW 2 (WS): **P13C, P12B, P13A.**
Rep rows 1-2 7 times more.
ROW 17: **K13D, K12E, K13D.**
ROW 18: **P13D, P12E, P13D.**
Rep rows 17-18 7 times more.
ROW 33: **K13C, K12B, K13A.**
ROW 34: **P13A, P12B, P13C.**
Rep rows 33-34 7 times more.
(48 rows)
Bind (cast) off.

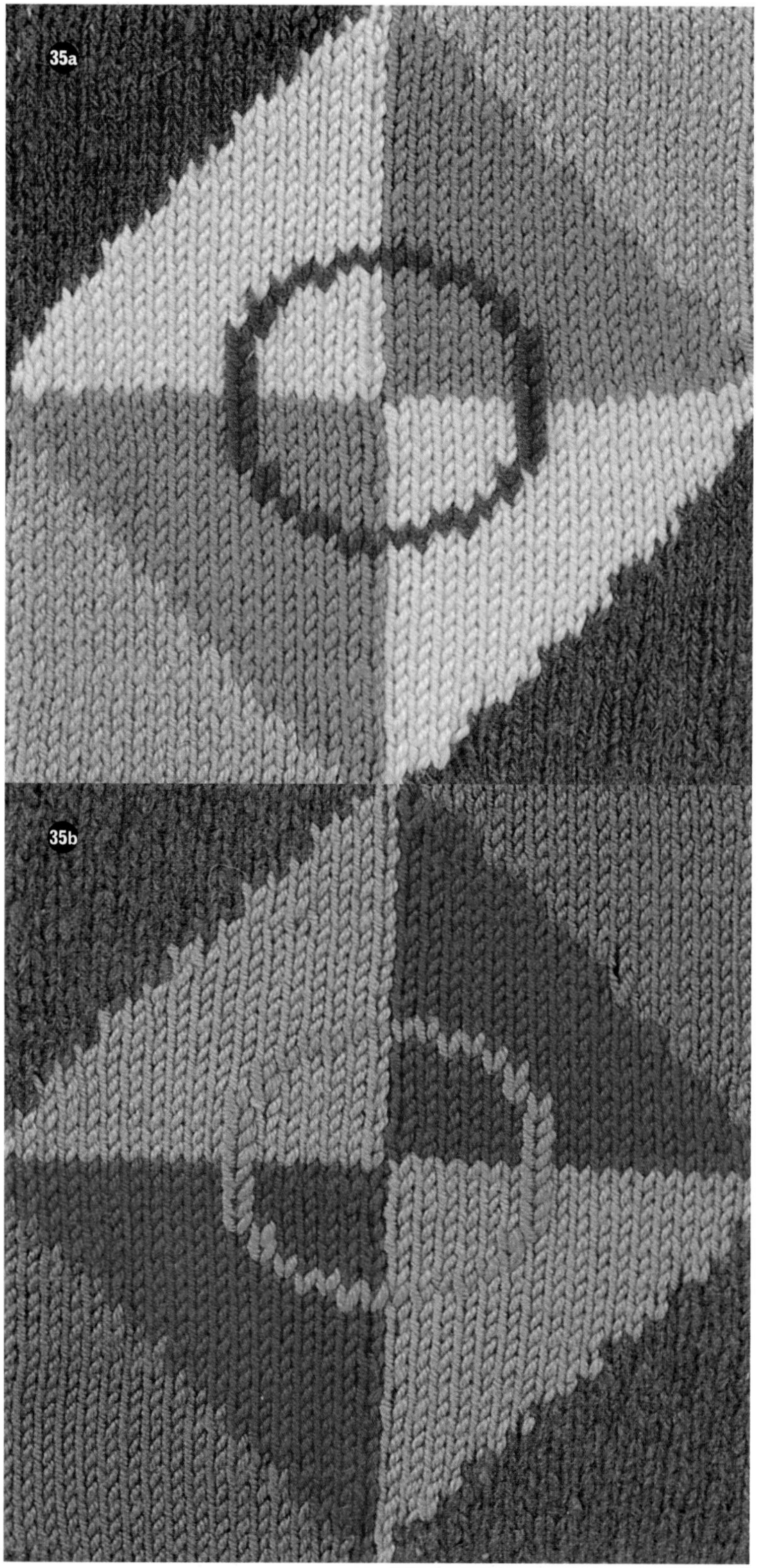

㉟ Ravenna

SIZE

6in × 6in (15cm × 15cm)

MATERIALS

1 pair US 5 (3.75mm/No. 9) needles

35a First colorway (×31 ⊞ ▣)

Rowan Wool Cotton
1¾oz (50g) balls

□	pale yellow (B)	1/16
■	green (C)	1/16
■	violet (D)	1/16
■	magenta (E)	1/50

Rowan Rowanspun DK
1¾oz (50g) hanks

■	purple tweed (A)	1/16

□ K on RS, P on WS

35b Second colorway (×28 ▣)

Rowan Wool Cotton
1¾oz (50g) balls

rose pink (B)	1/16
magenta (C)	1/16
mid blue (D)	1/16
green (E)	1/50

Rowan Rowanspun DK
1¾oz (50g) hanks

blue tweed (A)	1/16

KNIT

Cast on 40 sts and work until chart row 50 completed.
Bind (cast) off sts.

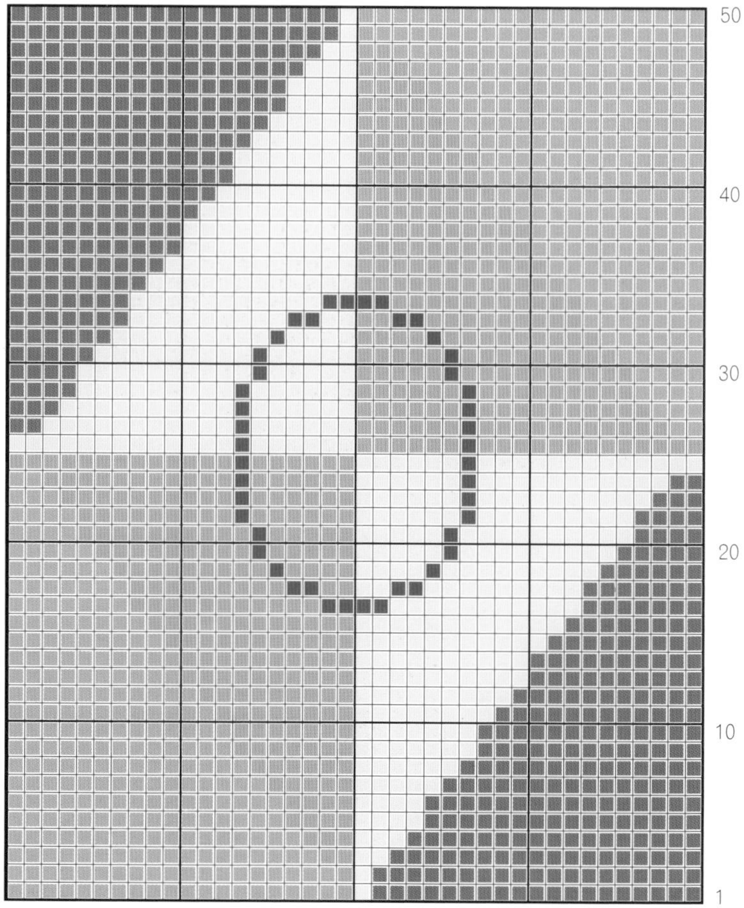

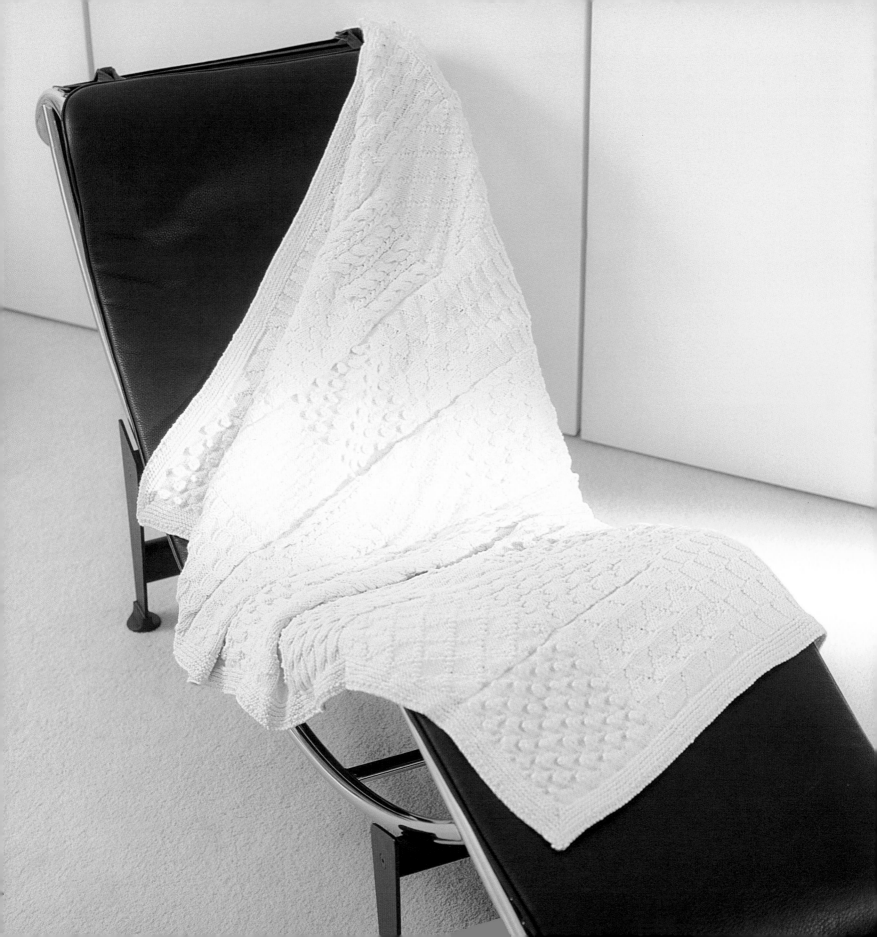

sampler

I designed this afghan especially for knitters who want to experiment with a range of textured stitches instead of color. Consequently there are many opportunities to try techniques such as cabling, bobbles and seed (moss) stitch. There is an underlying theme of the beach in this afghan. For example, cables imitate shell patterns and ropes; bobbles suggest pebbles and stones, and seed (moss) stitch patterns bring to mind sand swirls along the water's edge. A new version of basketweave stitch is used to suggest sea walls. Variations could be introduced by substituting a shade of yarn of your own choosing or by using a mixture of colors to give more of a patchwork effect. The patterning on Sampler is rich in texture, but could be lightened by the introduction of plain stockinette (stocking) stitch squares, interspersed between the textured squares. In fact, this afghan provides the adventurous knitter with many opportunities to experiment.

SIZE
71in x 58in (180cm x 148cm)

MATERIALS
1 pair US 5 (3.75mm/No. 9) needles
2 circular US 3 (3.25mm/No. 10)
   needles 39in (100cm) length
Cable needle

Yarn
Rowan Handknit DK Cotton
1¾oz (50g) balls
   cream   55

Quantities given for individual squares are approximate fractions of a ball.

GAUGE (TENSION)
22 sts and 30 rows to 4in (10cm) measured over reverse stockinette (stocking) stitch using US 5 (3.75mm/No. 9) needles.

ABBREVIATIONS
See page 127.

FINISHING
The sizes given for the finished afghan and individual squares are approximate. The number of stitches in a row, and the number of rows in a square differ in some instances. Therefore, when sewing pieces together, ease the extra stitches or extra rows into the adjoining square.

Finish the individual squares using a damp finishing process: pin the squares out flat onto a damp towel. Place a second damp towel on top of the squares, and leave to dry in room temperature. Sew the squares together, joining bound (cast) off edge of one square to the cast on edge of the next square, easing in stitches if necessary, to form vertical strips. Sew the vertical strips together, easing in rows if necessary, to create one block.

Edging

MATERIALS
2 circular US 3 (3.25mm/No. 10)
   needles 39in (100cm) length

Yarn
Rowan Handknit DK Cotton
1¾oz (50g) balls
   cream   2⅗

KNIT
With RS facing, pick up and knit 413 sts along the right-hand edge of the afghan.
Beg with a WS row cont to work in garter st (knit every row), inc 1 st at each end of all RS rows, until 9 rows are completed.
NEXT ROW (RS): (K1, P1) to last st, K1
Bind (cast) off sts knitwise.
Rep for left-hand edge of the afghan.
With RS facing, pick up and knit 327 sts along bottom edge of the afghan.
Rep edging as for right-hand and left-hand edges.
Rep for top edge of afghan.
Neatly sew border edges together.

Order of squares

36	42	40	44	38	44	40	42	36
37	43	41	45	39	45	41	43	37
38	44	36	42	40	42	36	44	38
39	45	37	43	41	43	37	45	39
40	42	38	44	36	44	38	42	40
41	43	39	45	37	45	39	43	41
40	42	38	44	36	44	38	42	40
39	45	37	43	41	43	37	45	39
38	44	36	42	40	42	36	44	38
37	43	41	45	39	45	41	43	37
36	42	40	44	38	44	40	42	36

QUANTITY OF SQUARES

36	Pebbles	10
37	Sand swirl	9
38	Sea wall	10
39	Cobbled stones	8
40	Twine	10
41	Pebble dash	8
42	Fishing nets	12
43	Mollusks	10
44	Sandy lines	12
45	Cables and twists	10

36 Pebbles

SIZE
6¾in × 6¾in (17cm × 17cm)

MATERIALS
1 pair US 5 (3.75mm/No. 9) needles

Single colorway (×10 ■)
Rowan Handknit DK Cotton
1¾oz (50g) balls
   cream   ½

KNIT
Cast on 39 sts.
Beg with a RS row, work 3 rows in reverse stockinette (stocking) stitch: (purl 1 row, knit 1 row, purl 1 row).
Pattern repeat:
ROW 4 (WS): K7, (P1, K5) 5 times, K2.
ROW 5 (RS): P4, (mb, P2, K1, P2) 5 times, mb, P4.
ROW 6 (WS): Knit.
ROW 7 (RS): Purl.
Rep the last 2 rows once more.
ROW 10 (WS): K4, (P1, K5) 5 times, P1, K4.
ROW 11 (RS): P4, (K1, P2, mb, P2) 5 times, K1, P4.
ROW 12 (WS): Knit.
ROW 13 (RS): Purl.
ROWS 14–15: Rep rows 12–13 once more.
Rep rows 4–15 twice more.
Rep rows 4–14.
(50 rows)
Bind (cast) off sts.

37 Sand swirl

SIZE
6¾in × 6¾in (17cm × 17cm)

MATERIALS
1 pair US 5 (3.75mm/No. 9) needles

Single colorway (×9 ■)
Rowan Handknit DK Cotton
1¾oz (50g) balls
   cream   ½

KNIT
Cast on 37 sts.
ROW 1 (RS): P5, (K7, P3) 3 times, P2.
ROW 2 (WS): K7, (P6, K4) 3 times.
ROW 3 (RS): P3, (K6, P4) 4 times, P4.
ROW 4 (WS): K8, (P6, K4) twice, P6, K3.
ROW 5 (RS): As row 3.
ROW 6 (WS): As row 2.
ROW 7 (RS): As row 1.
ROW 8 (WS): (K4, P6) 3 times, K7.
ROW 9 (RS): P8, (K6, P4) twice, K6, P3.
ROW 10 (WS): K3, (P6, K4) 3 times, K4.
ROW 11 (RS): As row 9.
ROW 12 (WS): As row 8.
Rep rows 1-12, 3 times more.
Rep rows 1-2 once more.
(50 rows)
Bind (cast) off sts.

OPPOSITE: *This afghan depends upon texture rather than color to define the individual squares.*

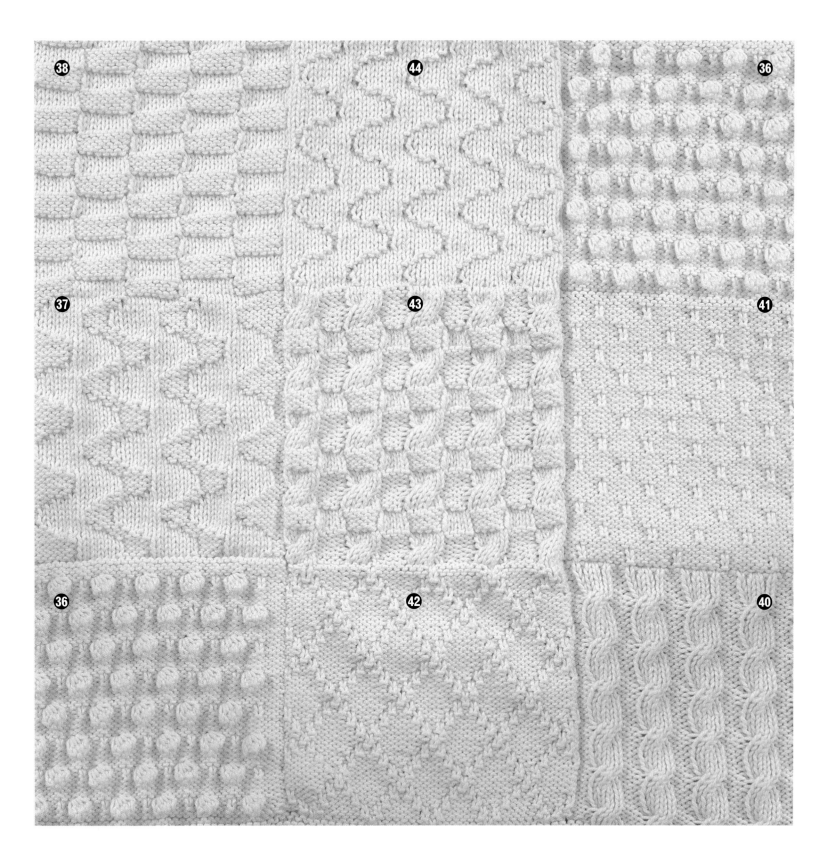

38 Sea wall

SIZE
6¾in × 6¾in (17cm × 17cm)

MATERIALS
1 pair US 5 (3.75mm/No. 9) needles

Single colorway (×10 ■)
Rowan Handknit DK Cotton
1¾oz (50g) balls
cream   ½

KNIT
Cast on 37 sts.
ROW 1 (RS): P8, (K7, P7) twice, P1.
ROW 2 (WS): K8, (P7, K7) twice, K1.
ROW 3 (RS): As row 1.
ROW 4 (WS): As row 2.
ROW 5 (RS): K8, (P7, K7) twice, K1.
ROW 6 (WS): P8, (K7, P7) twice, P1.
ROW 7 (RS): As row 5.
ROW 8 (WS): As row 6.
Rep rows 1-8, 5 times more.
Rep rows 1-4 once more.
(52 rows)
Bind (cast) off sts.

39 Cobbled stones

SIZE
6¾in × 6¾in (17cm × 17cm)

MATERIALS
1 pair US 5 (3.75mm/No. 9) needles

Single colorway (×8 ■)
Rowan Handknit DK Cotton
1¾oz (50g) balls
cream   ½

KNIT
Cast on 38 sts.
ROW 1 (RS): K3, (P2, K4) 5 times, P2, K3.
ROW 2 (WS): P3, (K2, P4) 5 times, K2, P3.
ROW 3 (RS): As row 1
ROW 4 (WS): (P2, K1) 12 times, P2.
ROW 5 (RS): (K2, P1) 12 times, K2.
ROW 6 (WS): (K2, P4) 6 times, K2.
ROW 7 (RS): (P2, K4) 6 times, P2.
ROW 8 (WS): As row 6.
ROW 9 (RS): As row 7.
ROW 10 (WS): As row 4.
ROW 11 (RS): As row 5.
ROW 12 (WS): As row 2.
Rep rows 1-12, 3 times more.
Rep rows 1-2 once more.
(50 rows)
Bind (cast) off sts.

40 Twine

SIZE
6¾in × 6¾in (17cm × 17cm)

MATERIALS
1 pair US 5 (3.75mm/No. 9) needles
Cable needle

Single colorway (×10 ■)
Rowan Handknit DK Cotton
1¾oz (50g) balls
cream   ½

KNIT
Cast on 38 sts.
ROW 1 (RS) (INC): P3, (K1, inc once in each of next 2 sts, K1, P3) 5 times *(48 sts)*.
ROW 2 (WS): K3, (P1, K1, P2, K1, P1, K3) 5 times.
ROW 3 (RS): P3, (K1, P1, K2, P1, K1, P3) 5 times.
ROW 4 (WS): As row 2.
ROW 5 (RS): P3, (c6b, P3) 5 times.
ROW 6 (WS): As row 2.
ROW 7 (RS): As row 3.
ROW 8 (WS): As row 2.
ROW 9 (RS): As row 3.
Rep rows 2-9, 5 times more.
NEXT ROW (WS) (DEC): K3, (P1, P2tog twice, P1, K3) 5 times *(38 sts)*.
(50 rows)
Bind (cast) off sts.

41 Pebbledash

SIZE
6¾in × 6¾in (17cm × 17cm)

MATERIALS
1 pair US 5 (3.75mm/No. 9) needles

Single colorway (×8 ■)
Rowan Handknit DK Cotton
1¾oz (50g) balls
cream   ½

KNIT
Cast on 37 sts.
ROW 1 (RS): Purl.
ROW 2 (WS): Knit.
ROW 3 (RS): P3, (K1, P5) 5 times, K1, P3.
ROW 4 (WS): K3, (P1, K5) 5 times, P1, K3.
ROW 5 (RS): As row 1.
ROW 6 (WS): As row 2.
ROW 7 (RS): P6, (K1, P5) 4 times, K1, P6.
ROW 8 (WS): K6, (P1, K5) 4 times, P1, K6.
Rep rows 1-8, 5 times more.
Rep rows 1-2 once more.
(50 rows)
Bind (cast) off sts.

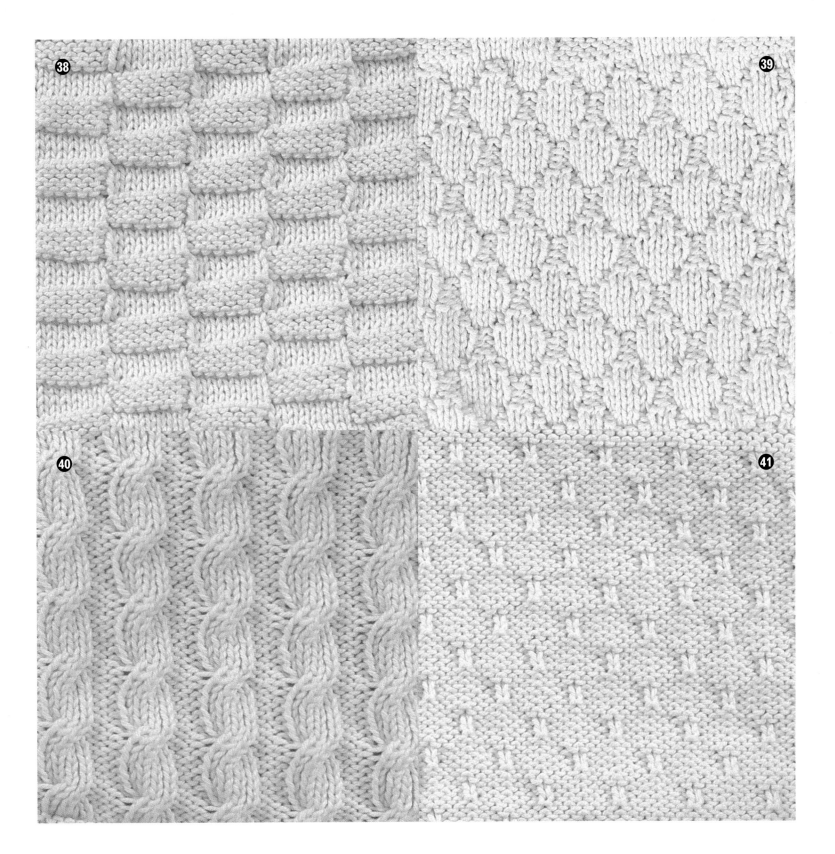

㊷ Fishing nets

SIZE
6¾in × 6¾in (17cm × 17cm)

MATERIALS
1 pair US 5 (3.75mm/No. 9) needles

Single colorway (×12 ◼)
Rowan Handknit DK Cotton
1¾oz (50g) balls
    cream   ½

KNIT
Cast on 39 sts.
ROW 1 (RS): P3, (K1, P7) 4 times, K1, P3.
ROW 2 (WS): K3, (P1, K7) 4 times, P1, K3.
ROW 3 (RS): P2, (K1, P1, K1, P5) 4 times, K1, P1, K1, P2.
ROW 4 (WS): K2, (P1, K1, P1, K5) 4 times, P1, K1, P1, K2.
ROW 5 (RS): P1, (K1, P3) 9 times, K1, P1.
ROW 6 (WS): K1, (P1, K3) 9 times, P1, K1.
ROW 7 (RS): K1, (P5, K1, P1, K1) 4 times, P5, K1.
ROW 8 (WS): P1, (K5, P1, K1, P1) 4 times, K5, P1.
ROW 9 (RS): (P7, K1) 4 times, P7.
ROW 10 (WS): (K7, P1) 4 times, K7.
ROW 11 (RS): As row 7.
ROW 12 (WS): As row 8.
ROW 13 (RS): As row 5.
ROW 14 (WS): As row 6.
ROW 15 (RS): As row 3.
ROW 16 (WS): As row 4.
Rep rows 1-16 twice more.
Rep rows 1-2 once more.
(50 rows)
Bind (cast) off sts.

㊸ Mollusks

SIZE
6¾in × 6¾in (17cm × 17cm)

MATERIALS
1 pair US 5 (3.75mm/No. 9) needles
Cable needle

Single colorway (×10 ◼)
Rowan Handknit DK Cotton
1¾oz (50g) balls
    cream   ½

KNIT
Cast on 38 sts.
ROW 1 (RS) (INC): K3, m1, K2, P4 (K2, m1, K2, P4) 3 times, K2, m1, K3 *(43 sts)*.
ROW 2 (WS): P6, K4, (P5, K4) 3 times, P6.
ROW 3 (RS): K6, P4, (K5, P4) 3 times, K6.
ROW 4 (WS): As row 2.
ROW 5 (RS): K1, (c5b, P4) 4 times, c5b, K1.
ROW 6 (WS): As row 2.
ROW 7 (RS): As row 3.
ROW 8 (WS): As row 2.
ROW 9 (RS): P6, (K4, P5) 4 times, P1.
ROW 10 (WS): K6, (P4, K5) 4 times, K1.
ROW 11 (RS): As row 9.
ROW 12 (WS): As row 10.
ROW 13 (RS): As row 3.
Rep rows 2-13, 3 times more.
Rep rows 2-7 once more.
NEXT ROW (WS) (DEC): P2, P2tog, P2, K4 (P2, P2tog, P1, K4) 3 times, P2, P2tog, P2 *(38 sts)*.
(56 rows)
Bind (cast) off sts.

㊹ Sandy lines

SIZE
6¾in × 6¾in (17cm × 17cm)

MATERIALS
1 pair US 5 (3.75mm/No. 9) needles

Single colorway (×12 ◼)
Rowan Handknit DK Cotton
1¾oz (50g) balls
    cream   ½

KNIT
Cast on 38 sts.
ROW 1 (RS): K3, (P3, K4) 5 times.
ROW 2 (WS): P3, (K1, P6) 5 times.
ROW 3 (RS): K7, (P1, K6) 4 times, P1, K2.
ROW 4 (WS): P2, (K1, P6) 5 times, P1.
ROW 5 (RS): As row 3.
ROW 6 (WS): As row 2.
ROW 7 (RS): K4, (P2, K5) 4 times, P2, K4.
ROW 8 (WS): (P6, K1) 5 times, P3.
ROW 9 (RS): K2, (P1, K6) 5 times, K1.
ROW 10 (WS): P7, (K1, P6) 4 times, K1, P2.
ROW 11 (RS): As row 9.
ROW 12 (WS): As row 8.
ROW 13 (RS): As row 7.
Rep rows 2-13, twice more.
Rep rows 2-12 once more.
NEXT ROW (RS): (K4, P3) 5 times, K3.
(49 rows)
Bind (cast) off sts.

㊺ Cables and twists

SIZE
6¾in × 6¾in (17cm × 17cm)

MATERIALS
1 pair US 5 (3.75mm/No. 9) needles
Cable needle

Single colorway (×10 ◼)
Rowan Handknit DK Cotton
1¾oz (50g) balls
    cream   ⅔

KNIT
Cast on 38 sts.
ROW 1 (RS) (INC): P3, (K1, inc once in each of next 3 sts, K1, P1, K2, P1) 3 times, K1, inc once into each of next 3 sts, K1, P3 (50 sts).
ROW 2 (WS): K3, (P8, K1, P2, K1) 3 times, P8, K3.
ROW 3 (RS): P3, (K8, P1, tw2l, P1) 3 times, K8, P3.
ROW 4 (WS): As row 2.
ROW 5 (RS): P3, (K8, P1, K2, P1) 3 times, K8, P3.
ROW 6 (WS): As row 2.
ROW 7 (RS): P3, (c8b, P1, tw2l, P1) 3 times, c8b, P3.
ROW 8 (WS): As row 2.
ROW 9 (RS): As row 5.
Rep rows 2-9, 5 times more.
NEXT ROW (WS) (DEC): K3, (P1, P2tog 3 times, P1, K1, P2, K1) 3 times, P1, P2tog 3 times, P1, K3 (38 sts).
(50 rows)
Bind (cast) off sts.

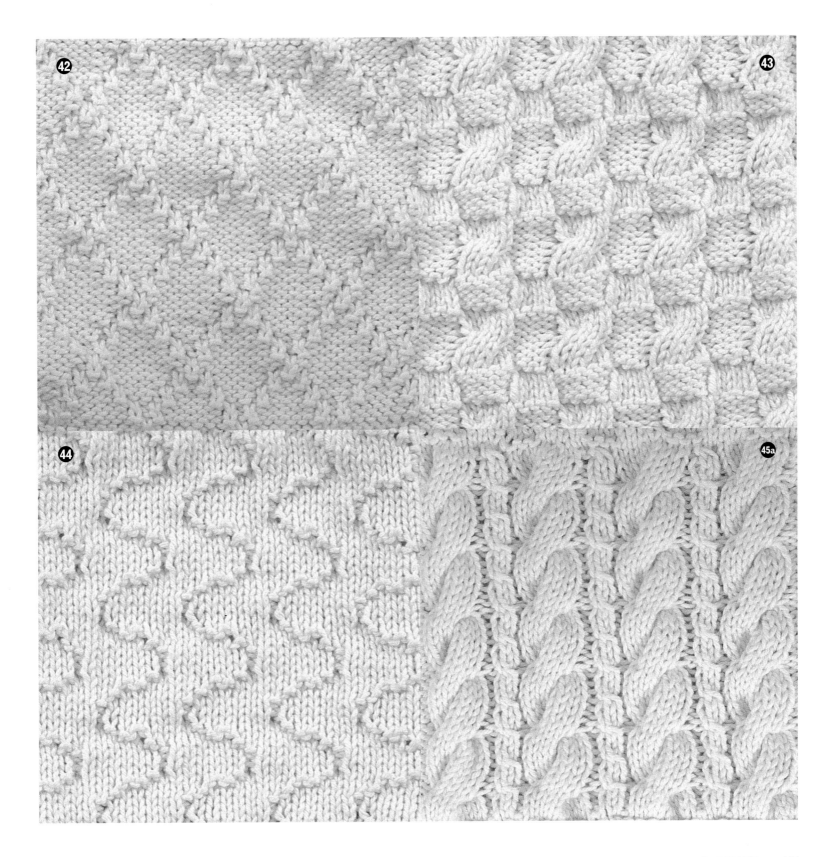

beside the seaside

The inspiration for this afghan came from my fond childhood memories of family trips to seaside resorts, which were only a short car journey away. Images of striped deck chairs, patterned windbreakers, rows of brightly colored beach huts, Punch and Judy shows and ice-cream and cotton candy stalls are all captured in this design. I remember walking along the beach, taking in the fresh air and looking out to sea to watch tiny, white sailing boats in the far distance bobbing along on the waves. Childhood pursuits, such as collecting jars of seashells, were always a joy. We would spend time wandering around the busy boatyards along the estuary, where piles of rusty chains and heavy ropes lay scattered among the shadows of the boats on the sand. I have used textured stitch patterns and beads to create the sand and shingle effects, and cables were the obvious choice to represent the piles of tangled rope. The fancy edging for this afghan is reminiscent of the pointed bunting strung across the busy side-streets.

SIZE
53in × 41in (135cm × 105cm)

MATERIALS
1 pair US 2 (3.00mm/No. 11) needles
1 pair US 2 (2.75mm/No. 12) needles
Cable needle

Yarn
Rowan Cotton Glace
1¾oz (50g) balls

soft yellow	2
bright yellow	1
pink	1
red	3
pale green	1
mid blue	3
light beige	4
white	5
navy blue	3
orange	1
cream	2

Rowan Linen Drape
1¾oz (50g) balls

turquoise	1

Quantities given for individual squares are approximate fractions of a ball.

Beads
⅛in (4mm) pebble beads

black	185
white	180
gunmetal	180
silver	210
red	35
green	35

Buttons
Beige ceramic buttons 10

GAUGE (TENSION)
25 sts and 34 rows to 4in (10cm) measured over stockinette (stocking) stitch using US 2 (3.00mm/No. 11) needles.

ABBREVIATIONS
See also page 127.

FINISHING
The sizes given for the finished afghan and individual squares are approximate. The number of stitches in a row, and the number of rows in a square differ in some instances. Therefore, when sewing pieces together, ease the extra stitches or extra rows into the adjoining square.

Press the individual squares using a damp cloth and warm iron. Sew the squares together, joining bound (cast) off edge of one square to the cast on edge of the next square, easing in stitches if necessary, to form vertical strips. Sew the vertical strips together, easing in rows if necessary, to create one block.

Edging

MATERIALS

1 pair US 2 (2.75mm/No. 12)
needles

Yarn
Rowan Cotton Glace
1¾oz (50g) balls
red (A)	1⅕
white (B)	1⅕
navy blue (C)	1⅕

KNIT

Cast on 6 sts.
ROW 1: **Knit.**
ROW 2 AND EVERY OTHER ROW: **Knit.**
ROWS 3, 5, 7, 9, 11: **Cast on 2 sts,
K to end.**
ROW 13: **Knit.**
ROWS 15, 17, 19, 21, 23: **Cast off 2 sts,
K to end.**
ROW 24: **Knit.**
Rep these 24 rows, changing color
as folls at the end of every 24 row
patt rep: A, B, C, B.
Cont until edging fits neatly around
all four edges of afghan.
Sew edging neatly onto afghan.

Order of squares

49	47	52	48	51	47	50
46	53b	46	54b	46	53a	46
52	47	51	48	50	47	49
46	53a	46	54a	46	53b	46
51	47	50	48	49	47	52
46	53b	46	54b	46	53a	46
50	47	49	48	52	47	51
46	53a	46	54a	46	53b	46
49	47	52	48	51	47	50

QUANTITY OF SQUARES

㊻	Ropes	16
㊼	Sand	10
㊽	Shingle	5
㊾	Beach huts	5
㊿	Punch and Judy	5
51	Sailing boat	5
52	Ice cream	5
53	Nautical stripe	
53a	First colorway	4
53b	Second colorway	4
54	Deckchair stripe	
54a	First colorway	2
54b	Second colorway	2

㊻ Ropes

SIZE

6in × 6in (15cm × 15cm)

MATERIALS

1 pair US 2 (3.00mm/No. 11) needles
Cable needle

Single colorway (×16 ◼)

Rowan Cotton Glace
1¾oz (50g) balls
light beige (A)	⅙
white (B)	⅕

KNIT

Cast on 38 sts using A.
ROW 1 (RS) (INC): **P5A, (K1B, B inc
once into each of the next 2 sts,
K1B, P4A) 4 times, P1A (46 sts).**
ROW 2 (WS): **K5A, (P6B, K4A)
4 times, K1A.**
ROW 3 (RS): **P5A, (K6B, P4A)
4 times, P1A.**
ROW 4 (WS): **Rep row 2.**
ROW 5 (RS): **P5A, (c6fB, P4A)
4 times, P1A.**
ROW 6 (WS): **Rep row 2.**
ROW 7 (RS): **Rep row 3.**
ROW 8 (WS): **Rep row 2.**
ROW 9 (RS): **Rep row 3.**
ROW 10 (WS): **Rep row 2.**
ROW 11 (RS): **Rep row 3.**
ROW 12 (WS): **Rep row 2.**
Rep rows 5–12, 5 times more.
Rep row 5 once more.
NEXT ROW (WS) (DEC): **K5A, (P1B,
P2togB twice, P1B, K4A) 4 times,
K1A (38 sts).**
(54 rows)
Bind (cast) off sts.

OPPOSITE: *Patterned and textured
images of the seaside are united
in this nostalgic knit.*

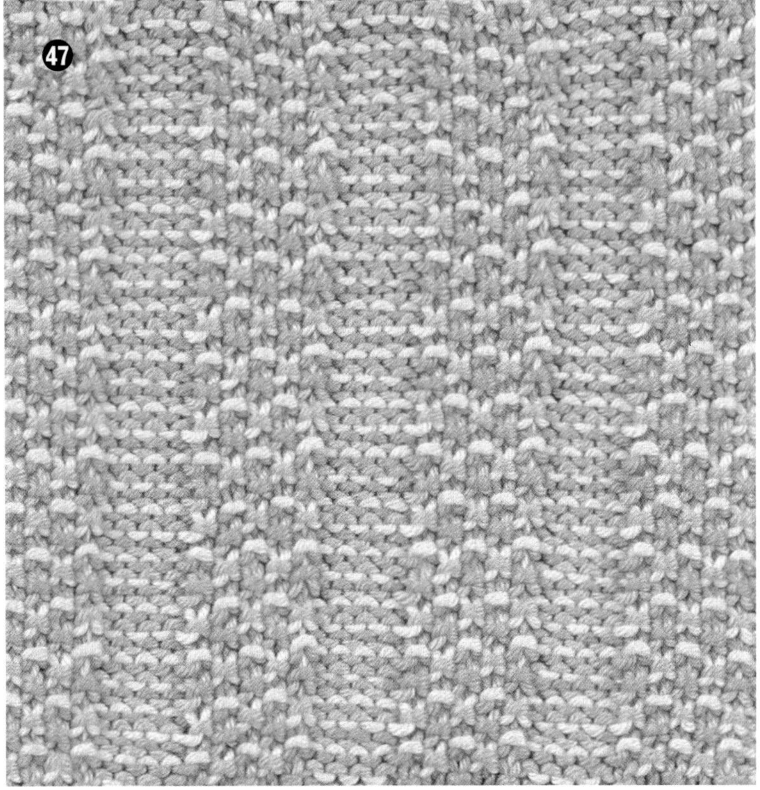

47 Sand

SIZE

6in × 6in (15cm × 15cm)

MATERIALS

1 pair US 2 (3.00mm/No. 11) needles

Single colorway (×10 ▣)
Rowan Cotton Glace
1¾oz (50g) balls

soft yellow (A)	1/10
light beige (B)	1/10
cream (C)	1/10

KNIT

Cast on 40 sts using A.
ROW 1 (RS): A, P4, [(K1, P1) twice, K1, P4] 3 times, (K1, P1) twice, K1, P4.
ROW 2 (WS): B, K5, (P1, K1, P1, K6) 3 times, P1, K1, P1, K5.
ROW 3 (RS): C, As row 1.
ROW 4 (WS): A, as row 2.
ROW 5 (RS): B, as row 1.
ROW 6 (WS): C, as row 2.
Rep the last 6 rows, 7 times more.
Rep rows 1-2 once more.
(50 rows)
Bind (cast) off sts.

48 Shingle

SIZE

6in × 6in (15cm × 15cm)

MATERIALS

1 pair US 2 (3.00mm/No. 11) needles

Single colorway (×5 ▣)
Rowan Cotton Glace
1¾oz (50g) balls

soft yellow (A)	1/12
light beige (B)	1/12
cream (C)	1/6

KNIT

Cast on 40 sts using A.
Seed (moss) st stripe patt rep.
ROW 1 (RS): B, (K1, P1) to last 2 sts, K2.
ROW 2 (WS): A, K2, (P1, K1) to end of row.
ROW 3 (RS): C, as row 1.
ROW 4 (WS): B, as row 2.
ROW 5 (RS): A, as row 1.
ROW 6 (WS): C, as row 2.
ROW 7 (RS): C, knit.
ROW 8 (WS): C, purl.
ROW 9 (RS): C, knit.
ROW 10 (WS): C, purl.
Beg with row 3 of the stripe patt rep, work as folls:
Work rows 3-10 once.
Work rows 1-10, 4 times.
Work rows 1-3 once.
(51 rows)
Bind (cast) off sts.

⑲ Beach huts

SIZE
6in × 6in (15cm × 15cm)

MATERIALS
1 pair US 2 (3.00mm/No. 11) needles

Single colorway (×5 ▦ ▣)
Rowan Cotton Glace
1¾oz (50g) balls

☐ soft yellow (A)	⅟₁₆
☐ pale green	⅟₁₆
☐ bright yellow	⅟₂₅
☐ pink	⅟₁₆
◼ red	
▨ mid	

Rowan Linen Drape
1¾oz (50g) balls

▨ turquoise	⅟₅₀

⅛in (4mm) pebble beads

● black	18
⊙ white	18
◉ gunmetal	18
⊙ silver	18

☒ Beige ceramic buttons   2

☐ K on RS, P on WS

KNIT

A in col order.
work until
leted.

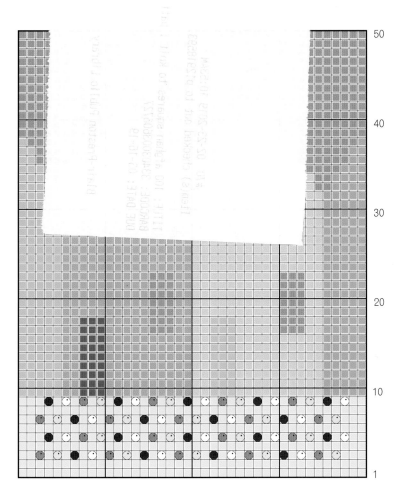

㊿ Punch and Judy

SIZE
6in × 6in (15cm × 15cm)

MATERIALS
1 pair US 2 (3.00mm/No. 11) needles

Single colorway (×5 ⊞ ▣)
Rowan Cotton Glace
1¾oz (50g) balls

□	soft yellow (A)	½
■	red	½
▨	mid blue	⅒
□	white	½₅
■	navy blue	⅕₀

Rowan Linen Drape
1¾oz (50g) balls

▨	turquoise	⅕₀

⅛in (4mm) pebble beads

●	black	19
⊙	white	18
◉	gunmetal	18
⊙	silver	18

□ K on RS, P on WS

⊟ P on RS, K on WS

KNIT
Thread beads onto A in col order.
Cast on 39 sts and work until
chart row 50 completed.
Bind (cast) off sts.

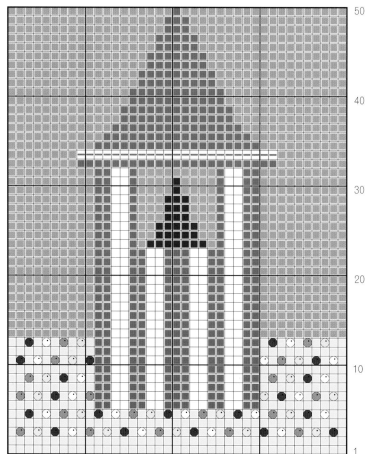

❺❶ Sailing boat

SIZE
6in × 6in (15cm × 15cm)

MATERIALS
1 pair US 2 (3.00mm/No. 11) needles

Single colorway (×5 ⊞ ▣)
Rowan Cotton Glace
1¾oz (50g) balls

▪ red	½₂₅
▪ navy blue	½₅₀
▨ orange	½₂₅
☐ bright yellow	½₂₅
▨ mid blue	¹⁄₁₀
▨ pink	½₂₅

Rowan Linen Drape
1¾oz (50g) balls

▨ turquoise	¹⁄₁₆

☐ K on RS, P on WS

KNIT
Cast on 40 sts and work until chart row 50 completed.
Bind (cast) off sts.

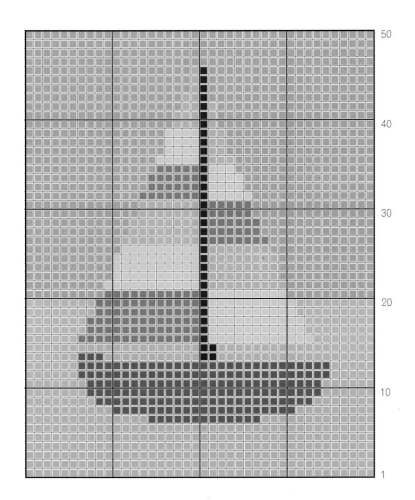

❺❷ Ice cream

SIZE
6in × 6in (15cm × 15cm)

MATERIALS
1 pair US 2 (3.00mm/No. 11) needles

Single colorway (×5 ⊞ ▣)
Rowan Cotton Glace
1¾oz (50g) balls

▨ mid blue (A)	¹⁄₆
▨ bright yellow (B)	¹⁄₁₆
▨ pink (C)	½₂₅
▨ pale green (D)	½₂₅
☐ cream (E)	½₂₅

⅛in (4mm) pebble beads

● red	7
● green	7
◉ silver	6

☐ K on RS, P on WS

⊟ P on RS, K on WS

KNIT
Thread 7 red beads onto C, 7 green beads onto D, then 6 silver beads onto E.
Cast on 40 sts and work until chart row 50 completed.
Bind (cast) off sts.

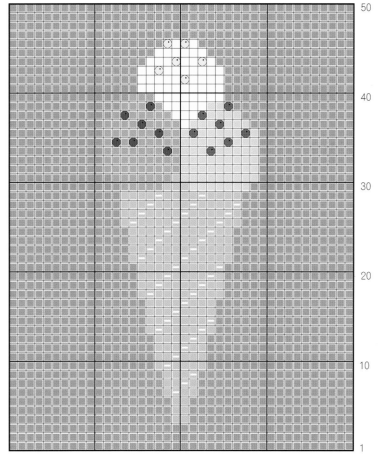

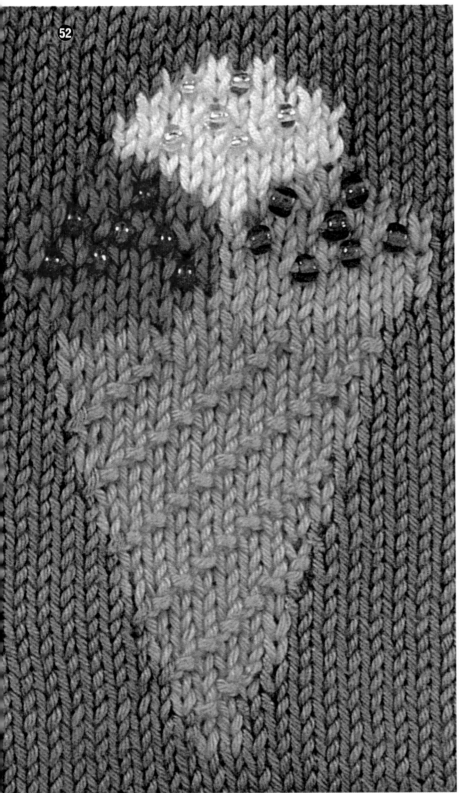

⑤ Nautical stripe

SIZE

6in × 6in (15cm × 15cm)

MATERIALS

1 pair US 2 (3.00mm/No. 11) needles

㊳ First colorway (×4 ▣)

Rowan Cotton Glace
1¾oz (50g) balls
    red (A)   ⅕
    white (B)   ⅛

㊳ Second colorway (×4)

Rowan Cotton Glace
1¾oz (50g) balls
    navy blue (A)   ⅕
    white (B)   ⅛

KNIT

Cast on 40 sts using A.
Beg with a RS row, work stripe
sequence in stockinette (stocking)
stitch as folls:
ROW 1-3: **A**
ROWS 4-6: **B**
ROWS 7-10: **A**
Rep rows 4-10, 5 times more.
Rep rows 4-6 once more.
Rep rows 1-3 once more.
(51 rows)
Bind (cast) off sts.

54 Deckchair stripe

SIZE

6in × 6in (15cm × 15cm)

MATERIALS

1 pair US 2 (3.00mm/No. 11) needles

54a First colorway (×2 ■)

Rowan Cotton Glace
1¾oz (50g) balls
    pink (A)   ⅕
    bright yellow (C)   1/12

Rowan Linen Drape
1¾oz (50g) balls
    turquoise (B)   1/16

54b Second colorway (×2 ■)

Rowan Cotton Glace
1¾oz (50g) balls
    orange (A)   ⅕
    bright yellow (B)   1/16

Rowan Linen Drape
1¾oz (50g) balls
    turquoise (C)   1/12

KNIT

Cast on 38 sts using A.

ROW 1 (RS): (K5A, K2B, K2C, K2B) 3 times, K5A.

ROWS 2 (WS): (P5A, P2B, P2C, P2B) 3 times, P5A.

Rep these 2 rows, 24 times more.
(50 rows)
Bind (cast) off sts.

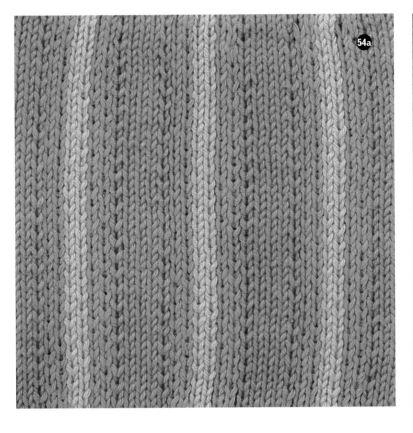

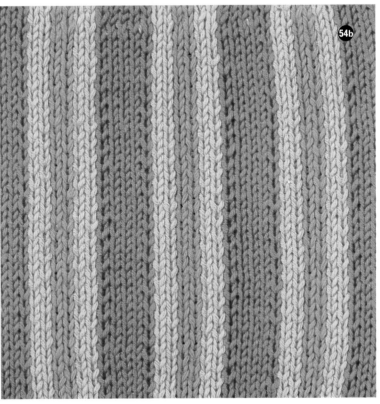

building blocks

I remember my mother putting me on the warm, sunny front porch of our family home, where, like many other young children, I used to spend happy hours playing with bright building blocks of wood and plastic. The primary colors of my original blocks have been changed in this design into a softer palette of green, violet and citrus shades, giving a more sophisticated look to a child-centered subject. A quiet, calm ambience is evoked through the use of these muted colors, providing a playmat which will soothe and comfort baby. I chose to use Wool Cotton for this afghan, not only because of its softness but also because it enhances stitch texture. Hexagons, squares, circles and triangles make up the design in seed (moss) stitch, and are mixed with bulky cables and reverse stockinette (stocking) stitch stripes and ribs.

SIZE

41in × 41in (105cm × 105cm)

MATERIALS

1 pair US 5 (3.75mm/No. 9) needles
2 circular US 3 (3.25mm/No. 10)
   needles 39in (100cm) length
Cable needle

Yarn

Rowan Wool Cotton
50g (1¾oz) balls

violet	3
pale yellow	4
cream	6
palest blue	2
mauve	3
green	3
palest yellow	1

Quantities given for individual squares are approximate fractions of a ball.

GAUGE (TENSION)

24 sts and 32 rows to 4in (10cm) measured over stockinette (stocking) stitch using US 5 (3.75mm/No. 9) needles.

ABBREVIATIONS

See also page 127.

FINISHING

The sizes given for the finished afghan and individual squares are approximate. The number of stitches in a row, and the number of rows in a square differ in some instances. Therefore, when sewing pieces together, ease the extra stitches or extra rows into the adjoining square.

Press the individual squares using a damp cloth and warm iron. Sew the squares together, joining bound (cast) off edge of one square to the cast on edge of the next square, easing in stitches if necessary, to form vertical strips. Sew the vertical strips together, easing in rows if necessary, to create one block.

Edging

MATERIALS

2 circular US 3 (3.25mm/No. 10)
   needles 39in (100cm) length

Yarn

Rowan Wool Cotton
1¾oz (50g) balls

cream	1⅘

KNIT

With RS facing, pick up and knit 260 sts along the right-hand edge of the afghan.
Beg with a WS row, cont to work in double seed (moss) stitch as folls:
ROW 1 (WS): **(K2, P2) to end of row.**
ROW 2 (RS): **Inc once into first st, K1, (P2, K2) to last 2 sts, inc once into next st, K1.**
ROW 3 (WS): **K1, (P2, K2) to last st, P1.**
ROW 4 (RS): **Inc once into first st, (P2, K2) to last 5 sts, P2, K1, inc once into next st, P1.**
Keeping the double seed (moss) st patt correct work 4 more rows, inc 1 st at each end of RS rows and

taking extra sts into the patt.
With WS facing cast off sts knitwise.
Rep for left-hand edge of afghan.
With RS facing, pick up and knit 256 sts along bottom edge of the afghan.
Rep edging as for right-hand and left-hand edges.
Rep for top edge of afghan.
Neatly sew border edges together.

Order of squares

58	61	55	62	56	61	57
59	56	60a	57	60b	58	59
57	62	58	61	55	62	56
60a	55	59	56	59	57	60b
56	62	57	61	58	62	55
59	58	60a	55	60b	56	59
55	61	56	62	57	61	58

QUANTITY OF SQUARES

55	Triangle	6
56	Hexagon	7
57	Circle	6
58	Square	6
59	Textured check	6
60	Lullaby	
60a	First colorway	3
60b	Second colorway	3
61	Multi stitch rib	6
62	Cozy cable	6

55 Triangle

SIZE
6in × 6in (15cm × 15cm)

MATERIALS
1 pair US 5 (3.75mm/No. 9) needles

Single colorway (×6 ⊞ ▣)
Rowan Wool Cotton
1¾oz (50g) balls
■ violet   ⅓

☐ K on RS, P on WS

⊟ P on RS, K on WS

KNIT
Cast on 39 sts and work until
chart row 50 completed.
Bind (cast) off sts.

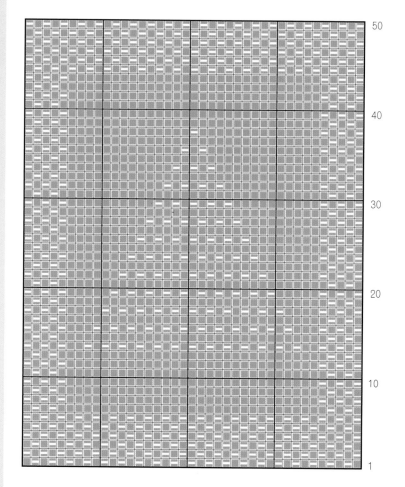

 Hexagon

SIZE
6in × 6in (15cm × 15cm)

MATERIALS
1 pair US 5 (3.75mm/No. 9) needles

Single colorway (×7 ▦ ▣)
Rowan Wool Cotton
1¾oz (50g) balls
☐ pale yellow   ⅓

☐ K on RS, P on WS

⊟ P on RS, K on WS

KNIT
Cast on 39 sts and work until chart row 50 completed. Bind (cast) off sts.

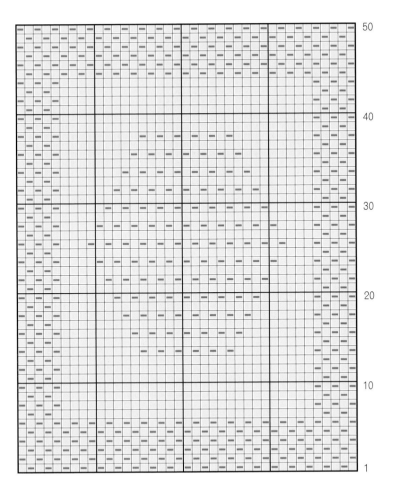

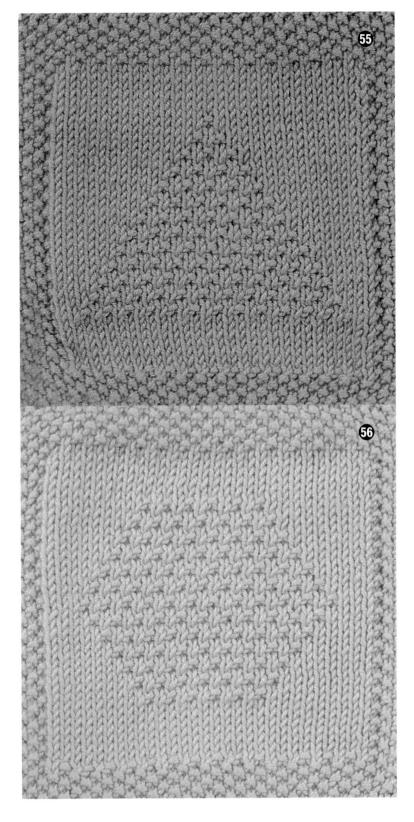

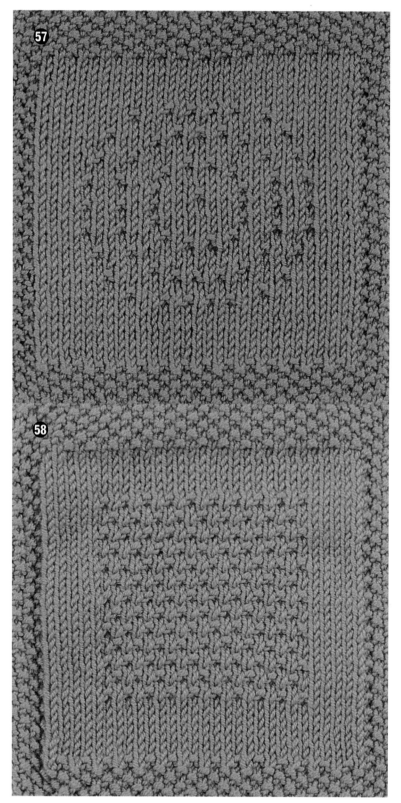

⑰ Circle

SIZE
6in × 6in (15cm × 15cm)

MATERIALS
1 pair US 5 (3.75mm/No. 9) needles

Single colorway (×6 ⊞ ▣)
Rowan Wool Cotton
1¾oz (50g) balls

▨ mauve   ⅓

☐ K on RS, P on WS

⊟ P on RS, K on WS

KNIT
Cast on 39 sts and work until chart row 50 completed. Bind (cast) off sts.

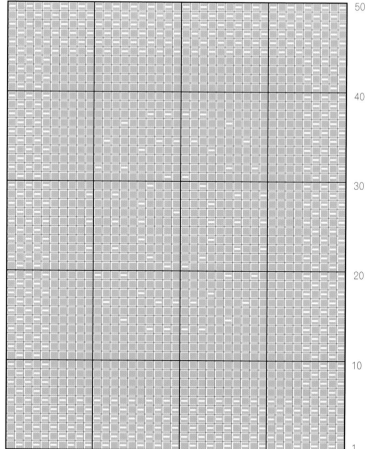

58 Square

SIZE
6in × 6in (15cm × 15cm)

MATERIALS
1 pair US 5 (3.75mm/No. 9) needles

Single colorway (×6 ▦ ▣)
Rowan Wool Cotton
1¾oz (50g) balls
▨ green   ⅓

☐ K on RS, P on WS

⊟ P on RS, K on WS

KNIT
Cast on 39 sts and work until chart row 50 completed.
Bind (cast) off sts.

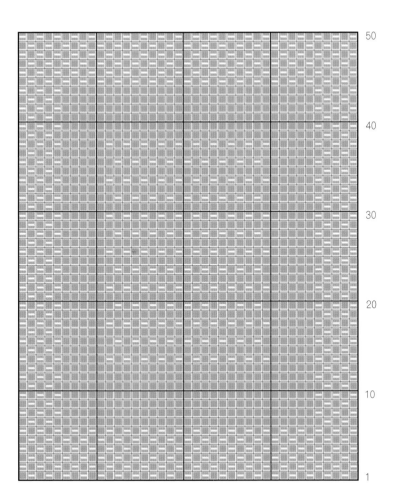

59 Textured check

SIZE
6in × 6in (15cm × 15cm)

MATERIALS
1 pair US 5 (3.75mm/No. 9) needles

Single colorway (×6 ▣)
Rowan Wool Cotton
1¾oz (50g) balls
   pale yellow (A)   ⅒
   cream (B)   ⅒
   palest blue (C)   ⅒

KNIT
Cast on 39 sts using A.
Work the square in the foll color sequence throughout: 1 row A, 1 row B, 1 row C.
ROW 1 (RS): **P9, [(K1, P1) 3 times, K1, P7] twice, P2.**
ROW 2 (WS): **K9, [(K1, P1) 3 times, K8] twice, K2.**
Rep rows 1-2, 4 times more.
ROW 11 (RS): **K1, P1, [(K1, P1) 3 times, K1, P7] twice, (K1, P1) 4 times, K1.**
ROW 12 (WS): **K1, P1, [(K1, P1) 3 times, K8] twice, (K1, P1) 4 times, K1.**
Rep rows 11-12, 4 times more.
These 20 rows set the pattern.
Rep the 20 row patt rep once more.
Rep rows 1-10 once more.
(50 rows)
Bind (cast) off sts.

60 Lullaby

SIZE
6in × 6in (15cm × 15cm)

MATERIALS
1 pair US 5 (3.75mm/No. 9) needles

60a First colorway (×3 ▣)
Rowan Wool Cotton
1¾oz (50g) balls
   palest blue (A)   ⅛
   pale yellow (B)   ⅛
   cream (C)   ⅒

60b Second colorway (×3 ▣)
Rowan Wool Cotton
1¾oz (50g) balls
   pale yellow (A)   ⅛
   palest blue (B)   ⅛
   cream (C)   ⅒

KNIT
Cast on 39 sts using A and beg with a RS row, work 4 rows in stockinette (stocking) stitch (knit 1 row, purl 1 row).
ROW 1 (RS): **B, (K1, P1) to last st, K1.**
ROW 2 (WS): **B, (K1, P1) to last st, K1.**
Rep rows 1-2 once more.
ROW 5 (RS): **C, as row 1.**
ROWS 6-9: **C,** work 4 rows in stockinette (stocking) stitch.
ROW 10 (WS): **A, (K1, P1) to last st, K1.**
ROW 11 (RS): **A, (K1, P1) to last st, K1.**
Rep rows 10-11 once more.
ROW 14 (WS): **B, as row 10.**
ROWS 15-18: **B,** work 4 rows in stockinette (stocking) stitch.
Rep rows 1-4 using C.
Rep rows 5-9 using A.
Rep rows 10-13 using B.
Rep rows 14-18 using C.
Rep rows 1-4 using A.
Rep rows 5-9 using B.
(49 rows)
Bind (cast) off sts.

❺ Multi-stitch rib

SIZE
6in × 6in (15cm × 15cm)

MATERIALS
1 pair US 5 (3.75mm/No. 9) needles

Single colorway (×6 ■)
Rowan Wool Cotton
1¾oz (50g) balls
palest yellow (A)	⅒
green (B)	1/12
palest blue (C)	1/12
mauve (D)	1/12

KNIT
Cast on 39 sts using A.
ROW 1 (RS): A, P7, [(K1, P1) twice, K1, P5] 3 times, P2.
ROW 2 (WS): A, K7, [(K1, P1) twice, K6] 3 times, K2.
ROW 3 (RS): A, as row 1.
ROW 4 (WS): B, as row 2.
ROW 5 (RS): B, as row 1.
Rep the last 2 rows.
*Rep rows 4-7 using C.
Rep rows 4-7 using D.
Rep rows 4-7 using A.
Rep rows 4-7 using B*.
Rep from * to * once more.
Rep rows 4-7 using C.
Rep rows 4-7 using D.
Rep rows 4-6 using A.
(50 rows)
Bind (cast) off sts.

❻ Cozy cable

SIZE
6in × 6in (15cm × 15cm)

MATERIALS
1 pair US 5 (3.75mm/No. 9) needles
Cable needle

Single colorway (×6 ■)
Rowan Wool Cotton
1¾oz (50g) balls
cream (A)	⅓

KNIT
Cast on 37 sts using A.
ROW 1 (RS) (INC): P4, (K1, inc once into next st, K1, inc once into next st, K1, P3) 4 times, P1 *(45 sts)*.
ROW 2 (WS): K4, (P7, K3) 4 times, K1.
ROW 3 (RS): P4. (K7, P3) 4 times, P1.
ROW 4 (WS): As row 2
ROW 5 (RS): P4, (c7b, P3) 4 times, P1.
ROW 6 (WS): As row 2.
ROW 7 (RS): As row 3.
ROW 8 (WS): As row 2.
ROW 9 (RS): As row 3.
ROW 10 (WS): As row 2.
ROW 11 (RS): As row 3.
ROW 12 (WS): As row 2.
Rep rows 5-12 4 times more.
Rep rows 5-9 once more.
NEXT ROW (WS) (DEC): K4, (P1, P2tog, P1, P2tog, P1, K3) 4 times, K1 *(37 sts)*.
(50 rows)
Bind (cast) off sts.

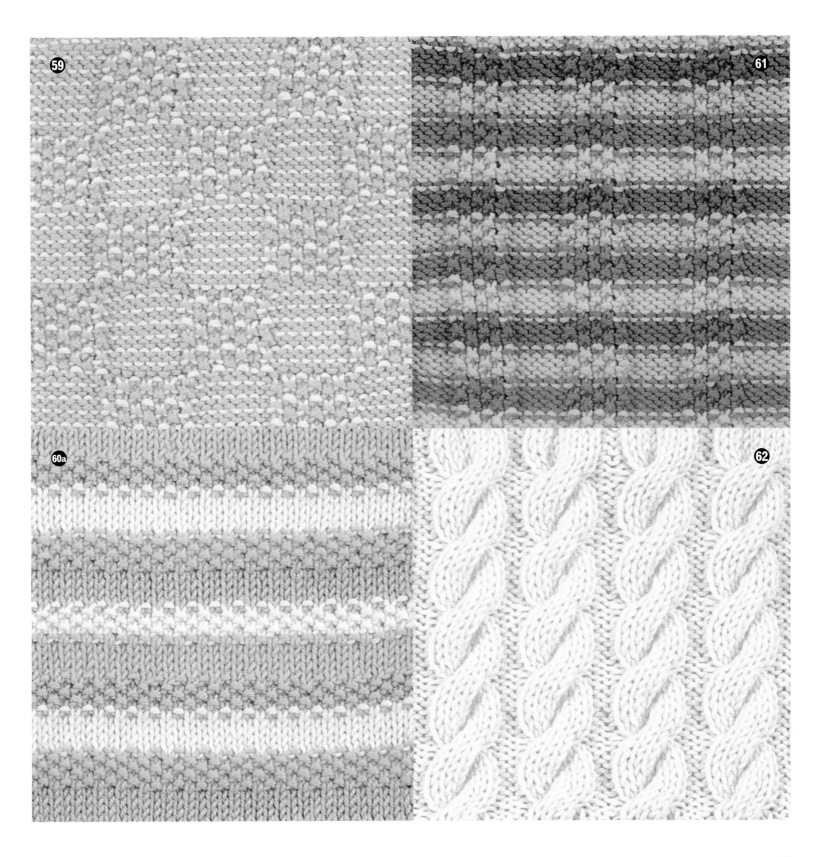

queen of hearts

The very first cushion collection that I ever designed was the Hearts Collection, based on one of my favorite shapes. The classic heart shape is one of the most widely used symbols in popular culture today, and is for many people a collectable image. In this design soft pastel cottons are embellished with glistening multi-colored beads and decorative textures. Delicate patterns in icing-sugar shades are laced with vibrant shots of orange and pink embroidered stitches. Designed to bring a sense of tranquility to a bedroom setting, this throw would look equally charming in a child's playroom. Selected squares from this design could be mixed and matched with different striped squares, checked squares or even plain knitted squares to create a pleasing variation on the original design.

The heart can be successfully combined with geometric shapes and it lends itself to infinite variation. I have enjoyed the challenge of finding new ways of interpreting this traditional and much-loved image in hand-knitting.

SIZE

85in × 59in (214cm × 148cm)

MATERIALS

1 pair US 5 (3.75mm/No. 9) needles
2 circular US 3 (3.25mm/No. 10)
  needles 39in (100cm) length

Yarn

Rowan Handknit DK Cotton
1¾oz (50g) balls

pink	4
apricot	8
pale gray	6
lilac	6
pale yellow	7
lime	5
green	3
mid blue	7
orange	3
mid yellow	5
bright yellow	1

Quantities given for individual squares are approximate fractions of a ball.

Beads

³⁄₁₆in (5mm) pebble beads

blue	840
pink	396
silver	375

GAUGE (TENSION)

22 sts and 30 rows to 4in (10cm) measured over stockinette (stocking) stitch using US 5 (3.75mm/No. 9) needles.

NOTE

Single stitch outlines on squares ⑥⑦ ⑥⑧ ⑥⑨ and ⑦⓪ can be Swiss-darned after knitting (see page 123).

ABBREVIATIONS

See also page 127.

FINISHING

The sizes given for the finished afghan and individual squares are approximate. The number of stitches in a row, and the number of rows in a square differ in some instances. Therefore, when sewing pieces together, ease the extra stitches or extra rows into the adjoining square.

Press the individual squares using a damp cloth and warm iron. Sew the squares together, joining bound (cast) off edge of one square to the cast on edge of the next square, easing in stitches if necessary, to form vertical strips. Sew the vertical strips together, easing in rows if necessary, to create one block.

Edging

MATERIALS

2 circular US 3 (3.25mm/No. 10)
    needles 39in (100cm) length

Yarn

Rowan Handknit DK Cotton
1¾oz (50g) balls
    orange   2

KNIT

With RS facing, pick up and knit
481 sts along the right-hand edge
of the afghan.
Beg with a WS row cont to work
in garter stitch (knit every row) for
4 rows, inc 1 st at each end of all
RS rows.
Bind (cast) off sts knitwise.
Rep for left-hand edge of
the afghan.
With RS facing, pick up and knit
319 sts along bottom edge of
the afghan.
Rep edging as for right-hand and
left-hand edges.
Rep for top edge of afghan.
Neatly sew border edges together.

Order of squares

66	63	69	71	64a	63	68	71	70
67	70	65	66	67	69	65	64b	67
64a	71	68	63	70	71	66	63	69
65	69	67	64b	65	68	67	70	65
70	63	66	71	69	63	64a	71	68
67	68	65	70	67	66	65	69	67
69	71	64a	63	68	71	70	63	66
65	66	67	69	65	64b	67	68	65
68	63	70	71	66	63	69	71	64a
67	64b	65	68	67	70	65	66	67
66	71	69	63	64a	71	68	63	70
65	70	67	66	65	69	67	64b	65
64a	63	68	71	70	63	66	71	69

QUANTITY OF SQUARES

63	Candy stripe	14
64	Beaded heart	
64a	First colorway	7
64b	Second colorway	5
65	Checkerboard	15
66	Textured heart	12
67	Outlined hearts	15
68	Bead and lace heart	11
69	Embroidered heart	12
70	Embossed heart	12
71	Sugar stripes	14

63 Candy stripe

SIZE

6½in × 6½in (16.5cm × 16.5cm)

MATERIALS

1 pair US 5 (3.75mm/No. 9) needles

Single colorway (×14 ■)

Rowan Handknit DK Cotton
1¾oz (50g) balls
    pale yellow (A)   ⅙
    lilac (B)   ⅙

KNIT

Cast on 38 sts using A.
Working in stockinette (stocking)
stitch cont in stripe patt rep as
folls, beg with a RS row:
ROWS 1-3: A.
ROWS 4-6: B.
Rep rows 1-6, 7 times more.
Rep rows 1-3 once more.
(51 rows)
Bind (cast) off sts.

64 Beaded heart

SIZE
6½in × 6½in (16.5cm × 16.5cm)

MATERIALS
1 pair US 5 (3.75mm/No. 9) needles

64a First colorway (×7 ▦ ▣)
Rowan Handknit DK Cotton
1¾oz (50g) balls
☐ pink (A)   ⅙
☐ apricot (B)   ⅙

³⁄₁₆in (5mm) pebble beads
● blue   75

☐ K on RS, P on WS

⊟ P on RS, K on WS

64b Second colorway (×5 ▣)
1¾oz (50g) balls
   pink (A)   ⅙
   apricot (B)   ⅙

³⁄₁₆in (5mm) pebble beads
   silver   75

KNIT
Cast on 37 sts and work until
chart row 50 completed.
Bind (cast) off sts.

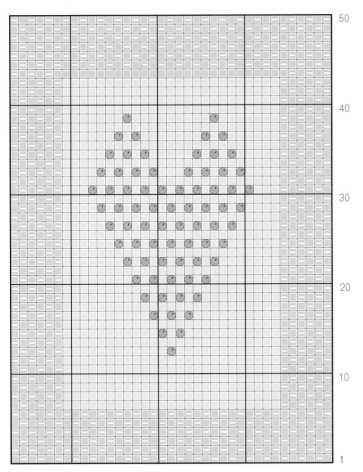

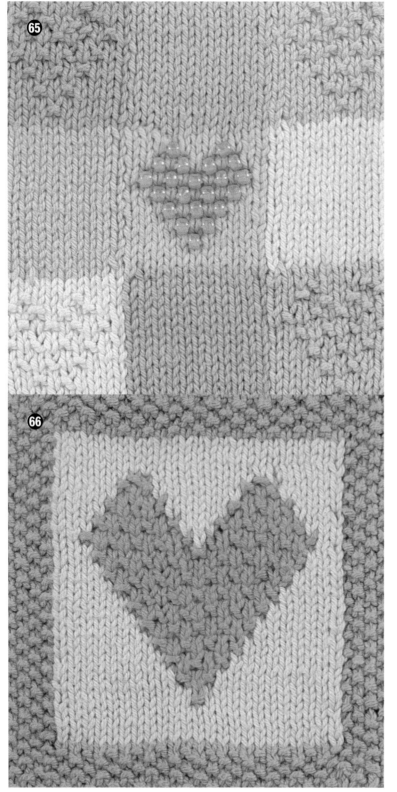

⑥⑤ Checkerboard

SIZE
6½in × 6½in (16.5cm × 16.5cm)

MATERIALS
1 pair US 5 (3.75mm/No. 9) needles

Single colorway (×15 ⊞ ▣)
Rowan Handknit DK Cotton
1¾oz (50g) balls

☐	pale gray	½2
▩	lilac	½2
☐	pale yellow	½2
☐	apricot	½2
☐	lime	½25

³⁄₁₆in (5mm) pebble beads

◉	blue	21

☐ K on RS, P on WS

⊟ P on RS, K on WS

KNIT
Cast on 39 sts and work until chart row 51 completed.
Bind (cast) off sts.

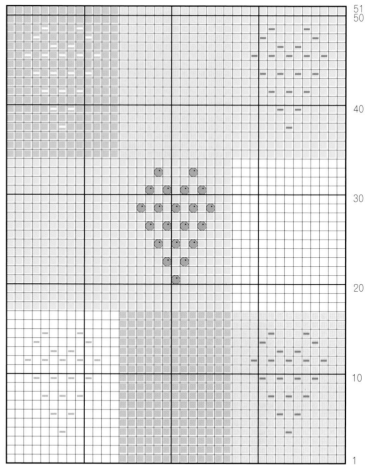

66 Textured heart

SIZE
6½in × 6½in (16.5cm × 16.5cm)

MATERIALS
1 pair US 5 (3.75mm/No. 9) needles

Single colorway (×12 ⊞ ▣)
Rowan Handknit DK Cotton
1¾oz (50g) balls

▨	green	⅙
☐	lime	¹⁄₁₂
▨	pink	¹⁄₁₀

☐ K on RS, P on WS

⊟ P on RS, K on WS

KNIT
Cast on 37 sts and work until chart row 50 completed. Bind (cast) off sts.

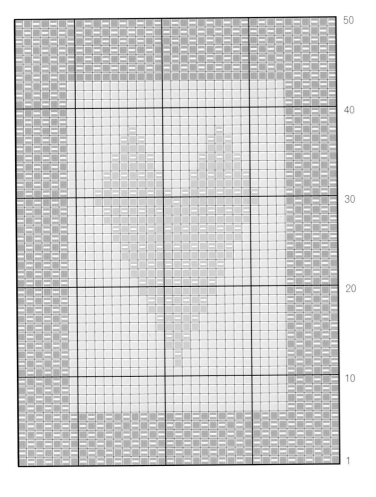

67 Outlined hearts

SIZE
6½in × 6½in (16.5cm × 16.5cm)

MATERIALS
1 pair US 5 (3.75mm/No. 9) needles

Single colorway (×15 ⊞ ▣)
Rowan Handknit DK Cotton
1¾oz (50g) balls

▨	lilac	¹⁄₁₂
☐	apricot	¹⁄₁₂
☐	pale yellow	¹⁄₂₅
▨	pale gray	¹⁄₁₂
▨	lime	¹⁄₁₂

☐ K on RS, P on WS

KNIT
Cast on 38 sts and work until chart row 50 completed. Bind (cast) off sts.

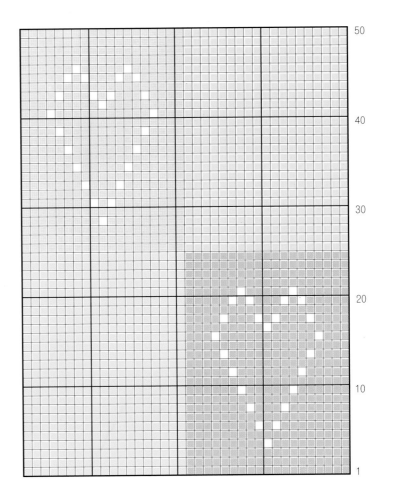

⓺ Bead and lace heart

SIZE
6½in × 6½in (16.5cm × 16.5cm)

MATERIALS
1 pair US 5 (3.75mm/No. 9) needles

Single colorway (×11 ⊞ ▣)
Rowan Handknit DK Cotton
1¾oz (50g) balls

▢ mid blue	⅓
▪ orange	¹⁄₁₆

³⁄₁₆in (5mm) pebble beads
⊙ pink   36

- ▢ K on RS, P on WS
- ⊟ P on RS, K on WS
- ◩ K2tog
- ⊙ Yarn forward

KNIT
Cast on 37 sts and work until chart row 50 completed. Bind (cast) off sts.

OPPOSITE: *The same basic heart shape is worked in beads, texture and color to provide variations on the theme.*

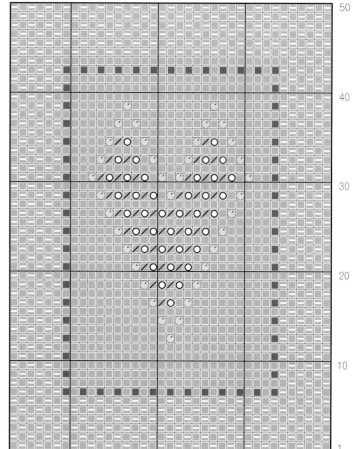

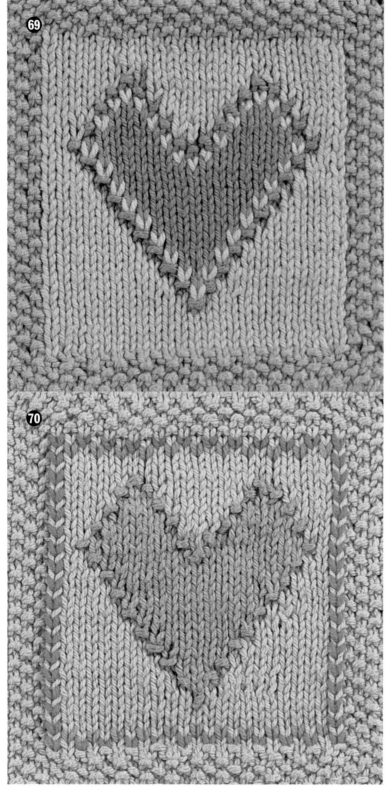

⑥⑨ Embroidered heart

SIZE
6½in × 6½in (16.5cm × 16.5cm)

MATERIALS
1 pair US 5 (3.75mm/No. 9) needles

Single colorway (×12 ⊞ ▣)
Rowan Handknit DK Cotton
1¾oz (50g) balls

▢	lilac	⅙
▢	pale gray	1/12
▢	mid blue	1/12
▢	apricot	1/25

▢ K on RS, P on WS

⊟ P on RS, K on WS

KNIT
Cast on 37 sts and work until chart row 50 completed. Bind (cast) off sts.

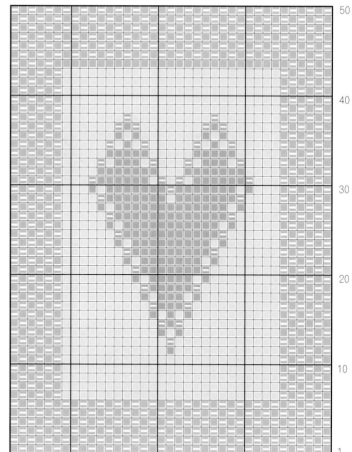

❼⓿ Embossed heart

SIZE

6½in × 6½in (16.5cm × 16.5cm)

MATERIALS

1 pair US 5 (3.75mm/No. 9) needles

Single colorway (×12 ▦ ▣)

Rowan Handknit DK Cotton
1¾oz (50g) balls

☐ mid yellow	¼
▨ orange	⅟25
☐ pink	⅟50
▥ green	⅟25
☐ lilac	⅟12

☐ K on RS, P on WS

⊟ P on RS, K on WS

KNIT

Cast on 37 sts and work until chart row 50 completed.
Bind (cast) off sts.

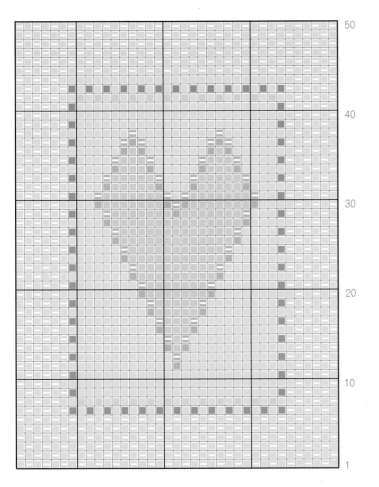

❼❶ Sugar stripes

SIZE

6½in × 6½in (16.5cm × 16.5cm)

MATERIALS

1 pair US 5 (3.75mm/No. 9) needles

Single colorway (×14 ▣)

Rowan Handknit DK Cotton
1¾oz (50g) balls

pale yellow (A)	⅟2
lime (B)	⅟2
bright yellow (C)	⅟25
apricot (D)	⅟2
pale gray (E)	⅟16

ROWS 1-2: **A.**
ROWS 3-5: **B.**
ROW 6: **C.**
ROWS 7-9: **D.**
ROWS 10-12: **E.**
ROW 13: **C.**
ROWS 14-16: **A.**
Rep rows 3-16 twice more.
Rep rows 3-8 once more.
(50 rows)
Bind (cast) off sts.

KNIT

Cast on 38 sts using A. Working in stockinette (stocking) stitch cont in stripe patt rep as folls, beg with a RS row:

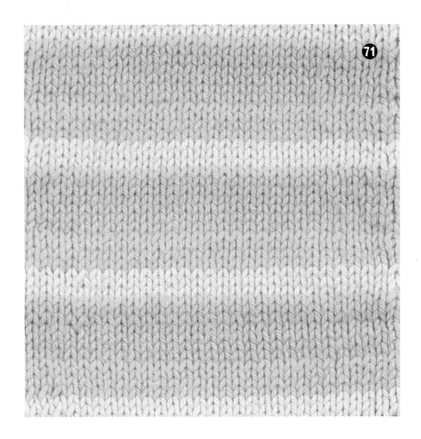

picnic

I have always enjoyed using denim yarn in my hand knitting. It is an extremely versatile yarn, easy to wash and maintain and it is very hard-wearing. The beauty of denim is that it fades after washing, just like denim jeans. This made it a very good choice of yarn for an afghan that can be used indoors and outdoors. I have used three different shades of denim in a mixture of textured stripes and squares, and the addition of silver and pearl beads adds extra sparkle. I imagine that, as the name implies, this afghan could be used for family outings and al fresco meals.

Because of the special washing requirements for denim yarn, care needs to be taken if mixing and matching squares with other knitted squares in this book. Please refer to the individual notes on each square.

SIZE
64in × 64in (161cm × 161cm)

MATERIALS
1 pair US 6 (4mm/No. 8) needles
2 circular US 3 (3.25mm/No. 10)
    needles 39in (100cm) length
Cable needle

Yarn
Rowan Denim
1¾oz (50g) balls

dark denim blue	20
cream	28
mid denim blue	19

Quantities given for individual squares are approximate fractions of a ball.

Beads
³⁄₁₆in (5mm) pebble beads

silver	648
pearl	450

GAUGE (TENSION)
(before washing)
20 sts and 28 rows to 4in (10cm) measured over stockinette (stocking) stitch using US 6 (4mm/No. 8) needles.

ABBREVIATIONS
See page 127.

FINISHING
The sizes given for the finished afghan and individual squares are approximate. The number of stitches in a row, and the number of rows in a square differ in some instances. Therefore, when sewing pieces together, ease the extra stitches or extra rows into the adjoining square.

Do not press squares. Sew the squares together, joining bound (cast) off edge of one square to the cast on edge of the next square, easing in stitches if necessary, to form vertical strips. Sew the vertical strips together, easing in rows if necessary, to create one block.

Edging

MATERIALS

2 circular US 3 (3.25mm/No. 10)
needles 39in (100cm) length

Yarn

Rowan Denim
1¾oz (50g) balls
    cream (A)   1⅖
    dark denim blue (B)   ⅘

Beads

³⁄₁₆in (5mm) pebble beads
    silver   134
    pearl   134

KNIT

With RS facing and using A, pick up
and knit 333 sts along the right-
hand edge of the afghan.
Beg with a WS row work 3 rows in
garter stitch (knit every row), inc 1
st at each end of the RS row
(335 sts).
Thread 34 silver and 33 pearl
beads alternately onto B.
NEXT ROW (RS): B, inc once into first
st, k to last 2 sts, inc once into
next st, K1. *(337 sts)*
NEXT ROW (WS): B, purl.
NEXT ROW (RS): B, inc once into first
st, K2, (pb, K4) 66 times, pb, K1,
inc once into next st, K1. *(339 sts)*
NEXT ROW (WS): A, purl.
NEXT ROW (RS): A, inc once into first
st, purl to last 2 sts, inc once into
next st, P1. *(341 sts)*
NEXT ROW (WS): A, purl.
NEXT ROW (RS): A, inc once into first
st, purl to last 2 sts, inc once into
next st, P1. *(343 sts)*
Bind (cast) off sts knitwise
using B.
Rep for left-hand edge of
the afghan.
With RS facing and using A, pick up
and knit 328 sts along bottom edge
of the afghan.
Thread 34 pearl and 33 silver
beads alternately onto B.
Rep edging as for right-hand and

left-hand edges but change the
beaded row to the foll:
NEXT ROW (RS): B, inc once into
first st, K2, (pb, K4) 65 times, pb,
K1, inc once into next st, K1.
Rep for top edge of afghan.
Neatly sew border edges together.

Washing the afghan to enable shrinkage

Darn in the ends on the WS of the
work. Put the afghan inside a
wash-bag that can be secured,
and wash in a large washing
machine at a temperature of 70-80
degrees C (or hottest WHITES
wash). Wash separately from other
washing. Tumble-dry the afghan
for approximately 40 minutes (if
facility is available).
Re-shape and dry flat.

Order of squares

QUANTITY OF SQUARES

72 Sunshine		
72a First colorway	5	
72b Second colorway	4	
73 Cable and texture		
73a First colorway	14	
73b Second colorway	4	
74 Beaded circles		
74a First colorway	4	
74b Second colorway	4	
75 Basketweave	6	
76 Tweedy rib	10	
77 Summer stripe		
77a First colorway	4	
77b Second colorway	4	
78 Textured check	8	
79 Reverse stripe	8	
80 Apple pips	4	
81 Patio	2	

OPPOSITE: ***The simple color
palette is enhanced with texture,
pattern and beads to create a
dazzling throw.***

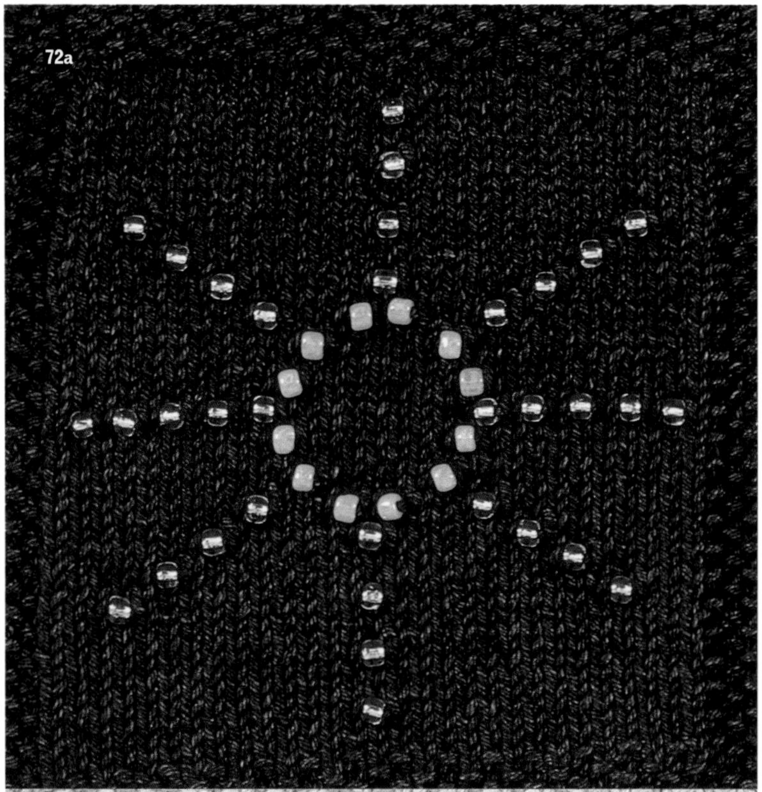

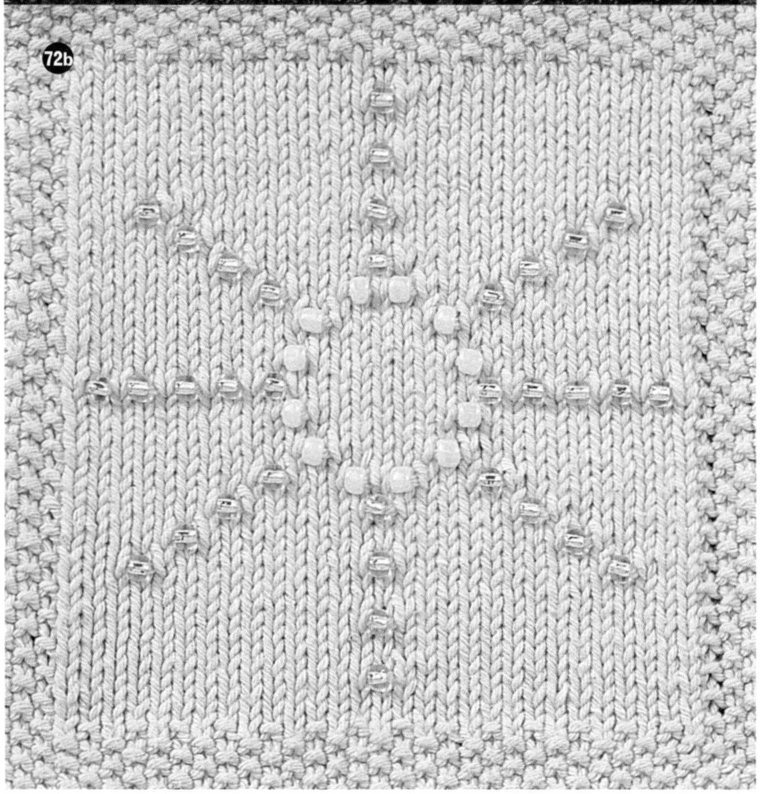

(72) Sunshine

SIZE
7in × 7in (18cm × 18cm)

MATERIALS
1 pair US 6 (4.00mm/No. 8) needles

(72a) First colorway (×5 ⊞ ▣)
Rowan Denim
1¾oz (50g) balls
■ dark denim blue ½

3/16in (5mm) pebble beads
⊙ silver 34
⊙ pearl 12

□ K on RS, P on WS

⊟ P on RS, K on WS

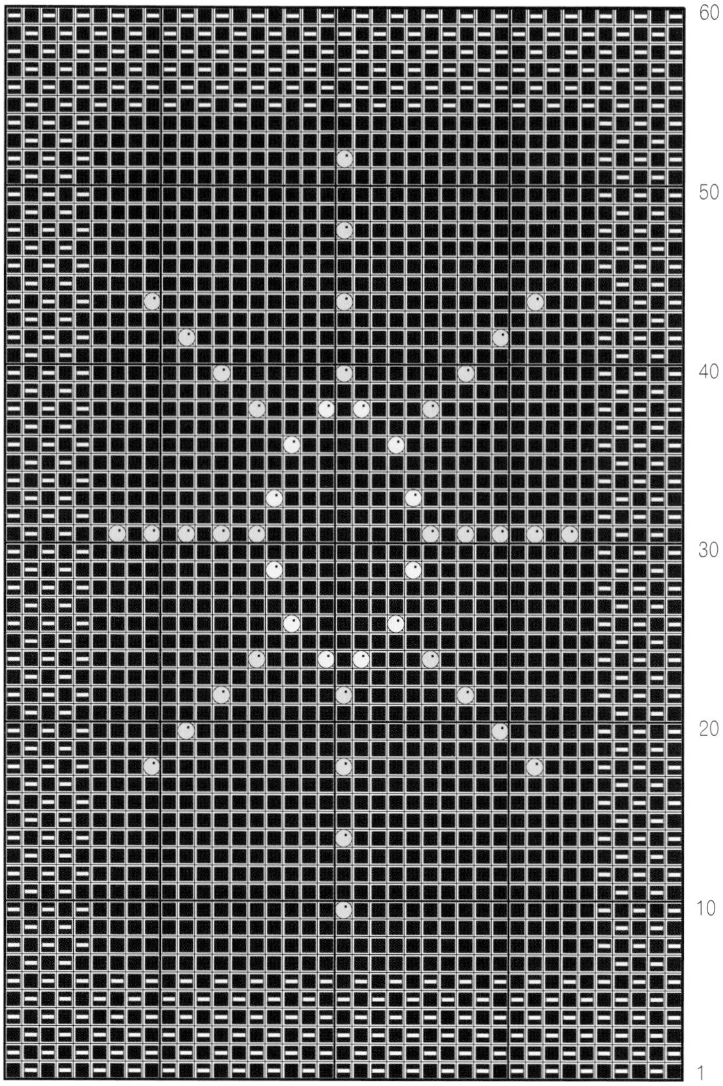

⑫ Second colorway (×4 ▣)

Rowan Denim
1¾oz (50g) balls
cream ½

³⁄₁₆in (5mm) pebble beads
silver 34
pearl 12

KNIT

Thread beads onto yarn before starting to knit in the foll sequence: 11 silver, 2 pearl, 1 silver, 4 pearl, 10 silver, 4 pearl, 1 silver, 2 pearl, 11 silver.

Cast on 39 sts and work until chart row 60 completed. Bind (cast) off sts.

Mixing and matching:
this square is not suitable for knitting up in other yarns.

⑬ Cable and texture

SIZE

7in × 7in (18cm × 18cm)

MATERIALS

1 pair US 6 (4.00mm/No. 8) needles
Cable needle

⑬ₐ First colorway (×14 ▣)

Rowan Denim
1¾oz (50g) balls
cream ³⁄₅

⑬ᵦ Second colorway (×4 ▣)

Rowan Denim
1¾oz (50g) balls
dark denim blue ³⁄₅

KNIT

Cast on 38 sts.
ROW 1: (RS) (INC): K1, P1, (K2, inc once into next 2 sts, K2, P1) 5 times, K1 (48 sts).
ROW 2: (WS): (K1, P1, K1, P6) 5 times, K1, P1, K1.
ROW 3: (RS): K1, P1, (K8, P1) 5 times, K1.
ROW 4: (WS): As row 2.
ROW 5: (RS): (K1, P1, K1, c6b, K1, P1, K1, c6f) twice, K1, P1, K1, c6b, K1, P1, K1.
✳Rep rows 2-3, 3 times.
Rep row 2 once more.
Rep row 5 once more ✳.
Rep from ✳ to ✳ 6 times more.
Rep rows 2-3 once more.
NEXT ROW (WS) (DEC): (K1, P1, K1, P1, P2tog twice, P1) 5 times, K1, P1, K1 *(38 sts)*.
(64 rows)
Bind (cast) off sts.

Mixing and matching:
this square can be knitted using other yarns, but the foll instruction must be changed from "Rep from ✳ to ✳ 6 times more" to "Rep from ✳ to ✳ 4 times more"
(48 rows).

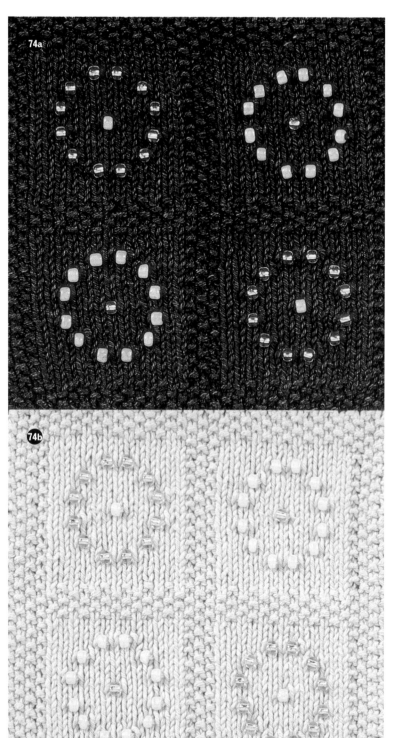

74 Beaded circles

SIZE
7in × 7in (18cm × 18cm)

MATERIALS
1 pair US 6 (4.00mm/No. 8) needles

74a **First colorway** (×4 ⊞ ▣)
Rowan Denim
1¾oz (50g) balls
■ dark denim blue   ½

³⁄₁₆in (5mm) pebble beads
⊙ silver   26
⊙ pearl   26

☐ K on RS, P on WS

⊟ P on RS, K on WS

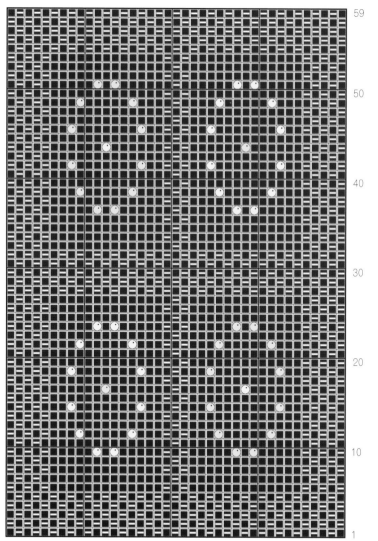

⁷⁴ᵇ Second colorway (×4 ■)

Rowan Denim
1¾oz (50g) balls
cream	½

Pebble beads 5mm
silver	26
pearl	26

KNIT

Thread beads onto yarn before starting to knit, in the foll sequence: 2 silver, 2 pearl, 2 silver, 4 pearl, 3 silver, 3 pearl, 4 silver, 2 pearl, 2 silver, 2 pearl, 2 silver, 2 pearl, 2 silver, 4 pearl, 3 silver, 3 pearl, 4 silver, 2 pearl, 2 silver, 2 pearl.
Cast on 39 sts and work until chart row 59 completed.
Bind (cast) off sts.

Mixing and matching:
this square is not suitable for knitting up in other yarns.

⑦⑤ Basketweave

SIZE

7in × 7in (18cm × 18cm)

MATERIALS

1 pair US 6 (4.00mm/No. 8) needles

Single colorway (×6 ■)

Rowan Denim
1¾oz (50g) balls
mid denim blue	½

KNIT

Cast on 37sts.
Basketweave patt rep:
ROW 1: (RS): **P6, (K5, P5) 3 times, P1.**
ROW 2: (WS): **K6, (P5, K5) 3 times, K1.**
ROWS 3-4: **Rep rows 1-2.**
ROW 5: (RS): **P6, (K2, P1, K2, P5) 3 times, P1.**
ROW 6: (WS): **As row 2.**
ROWS 7-8: **Rep rows 1-2.**
ROW 9: (RS): **K6, (P5, K5) 3 times, K1.**
ROW 10: (WS): **P6, (K5, P5) 3 times, P1.**
ROWS 11-12: **Rep rows 9-10.**
ROW 13: (RS): **K3, P1, K2, (P6, K2, P1, K2) 3 times, K1.**
ROW 14: (WS): **As row 10.**
ROWS 15-16: **Rep rows 9-10.**
Rep the 16 row patt rep twice more.
Rep rows 1-8 once more.
(56 rows)
Bind (cast) off sts.

Mixing and matching:
this square can be knitted using other yarns, but the foll instruction must be omitted "Rep rows 1-8 once more" *(48 rows).*

⑦⑥ Tweedy rib

SIZE

7in × 7in (18cm × 18cm)

MATERIALS

1 pair US 6 (4.00mm/No. 8) needles

Single colorway (×10 ■)

Rowan Denim
1¾oz (50g) balls
cream (A)	⅙
dark denim blue (B)	⅙
mid denim blue (C)	⅙

KNIT

Cast on 37 sts using A.
Work the reverse rib patt rep in the foll color sequence, changing color at the beg of every row:
Work 1 row B
Work 1 row C
Work 1 row A

Reverse rib patt rep:
ROW 1 (RS): **P6, (K1, P5) 5 times, P1.**
ROW 2 (WS): **K6, (P1 K5) 5 times, K1.**
Rep the 2 row patt rep 30 times in total.
(60 rows)
Bind (cast) off sts.

Mixing and matching:
this square can be knitted using other yarns, but the foll instruction must be changed from "Rep the 2 row patt rep 30 times in total" to "Rep the 2 row patt rep 25 times in total" *(50 rows).*

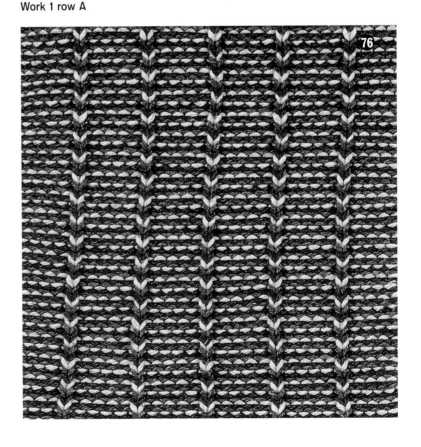

77 Summer stripe

OPPOSITE: *Denim yarns fade beautifully with every wash, so the more use your Picnic blanket gets, the more attractive it will become.*

SIZE

7in × 7in (18cm × 18cm)

MATERIALS

1 pair US 6 (4.00mm/No. 8) needles

77a First colorway (×4 ▦ ▣)

Rowan Denim
1¾oz (50g) balls

■	dark denim blue (A)	⅛
□	cream (B)	⅛
■	mid denim blue (C)	⅓

□ K on RS, P on WS

⊟ P on RS, K on WS

77b Second colorway (×4 ▣)

Rowan Denim
1¾oz (50g) balls

cream (A)	⅛
dark denim blue (B)	⅛
mid denim blue (C)	⅓

KNIT

Cast on 38sts.
Beg with a RS row work chart
rows 1-14, 4 times.
Rep chart rows 1-3 once more.
(59 rows)
Bind (cast) off sts.

Mixing and matching:
this square can be knitted using
other yarns but work as folls:
Beg with a RS row work chart
rows 1-14, 3 times.
Rep chart rows 1-10 once more.

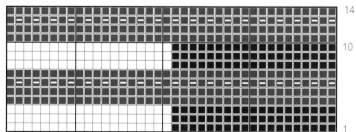

⑦⑧ Textured check

SIZE
7in × 7in (18cm × 18cm)

MATERIALS
1 pair US 6 (4.00mm/No. 8) needles

Single colorway (×8 ■)
Rowan Denim
1¾oz (50g) balls
   mid denim blue   ½

KNIT
Cast on 38 sts.
ROW 1 (RS): K3, (P2, K2)
8 times, P3.
ROW 2 (WS): As row 1.
ROW 3 (RS): P3, (K2, P2)
8 times, K3.
ROW 4 (WS): As row 3.
Rep rows 1-4, 13 times more.
Rep rows 1-2 once more.
(58 rows)
Bind (cast) off sts.

Mixing and matching:
this square can be knitted using other yarns but the foll instruction must be changed from "Rep rows 1-4, 13 times more" to "Rep rows 1-4, 11 times more" *(50 rows)*.

⑦⑨ Reverse stripe

SIZE
7in × 7in (18cm × 18cm)

MATERIALS
1 pair US 6 (4.00mm/No. 8) needles

Single colorway (×8 ■)
Rowan Denim
1¾oz (50g) balls
   dark denim blue (A)   ⅓
   mid denim blue (B)   ⅕

KNIT
Cast on 38sts using A.
ROW 1 (RS): A, purl.
ROW 2 (WS): A, knit.
ROW 3 (RS): A, purl.
ROW 4 (WS): B, knit.
ROW 5 (RS): B, purl.
ROW 6 (WS): B, knit.
ROW 7 (RS): A, purl.
ROW 8 (WS): A, knit.
ROW 9 (RS): A, purl.
ROW 10 (WS): A, knit.
ROW 11 (RS): B, purl.
ROW 12 (WS): B, knit.
ROW 13 (RS): B, purl.
ROW 14 (WS): A, knit.
ROW 15 (RS): A, purl.
ROW 16 (WS): A, knit.
ROW 17 (RS): A, purl.
Rep rows 4-17 twice more.
Rep rows 4-16 once more.
(58 rows)
Bind (cast) off sts.

Mixing and matching:
this square can be knitted using other yarns, but the foll instruction must be changed from "Rep rows 4-16 once more" to "Rep rows 4-9 once more" *(51 rows)*.

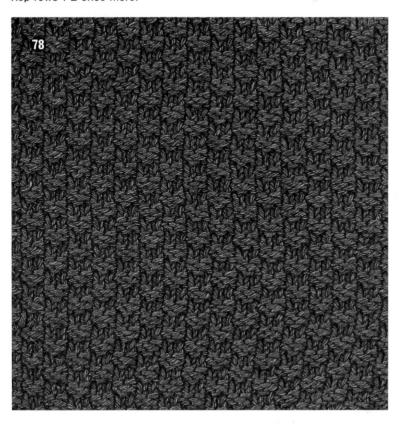

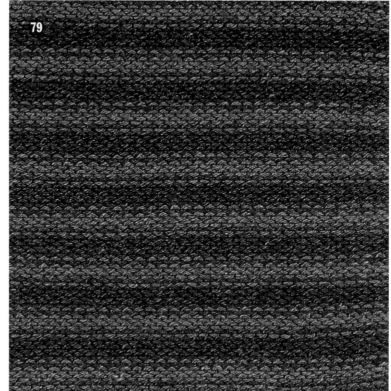

⑧⓪ Apple pips

SIZE

7in × 7in (18cm × 18cm)

MATERIALS

1 pair US 6 (4.00mm/No. 8) needles

Single colorway (×4 ■)

Rowan Denim
1¾oz (50g) balls
   cream   ½

KNIT

Cast on 37 sts.
Beg with a RS row, work 2 rows in stockinette (stocking) stitch (knit 1 row, purl 1 row).
ROW 1 (RS): K2, (P1, K3) 8 times, P1, K2.
ROW 2 (WS): Purl.
ROW 3 (RS): Knit.
ROW 4 (WS): Purl.
ROW 5 (RS): K4, (P1, K3) 8 times, K1.
ROWS 6-8: As rows 2-4.
Rep rows 1-8, 6 times more.
Rep rows 1-2 once more.
(60 rows)
Bind (cast) off sts.

Mixing and matching:
this square can be knitted using other yarns, but the foll instruction must be changed from "Rep rows 1-8, 6 times more" to "Rep rows 1-8, 5 times more" *(52 rows)*.

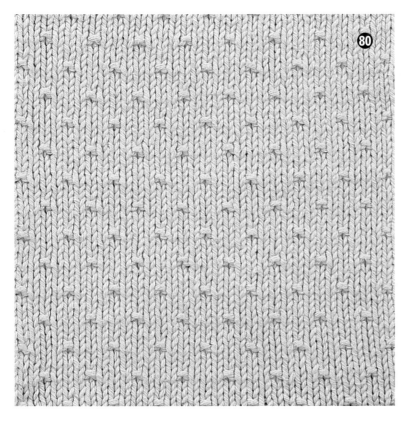

⑧① Patio

SIZE

7in × 7in (18cm × 18cm)

MATERIALS

1 pair US 6 (4.00mm/No. 8) needles

Single colorway (×2 ■)

Rowan Denim
1¾oz (50g) balls
   mid denim blue   ½

KNIT

Cast on 38 sts.
ROW 1 (RS): (K6, P1, K1) 4 times, K6.
ROW 2 (WS): P6, (K1, P7) 4 times.
ROWS 3-10: Rep rows 1-2, 4 times.
ROW 11 (RS): (P1, K1) to end of row.
ROW 12 (WS): (K1, P1) to end of row
ROW 13 (RS): As row 11.
ROW 14 (WS): As row 2.
ROW 15 (RS): As row 1.
ROWS 16-23: Rep rows 14-15, 4 times.
ROW 24 (WS): As row 12.
ROW 25 (RS): As row 11.
ROW 26 (WS): As row 12.
Rep rows 1-26 once more.
Rep rows 1-10 once more.
(62 rows)
Bind (cast) off sts.

Mixing and matching:
this square can be knitted using other yarns, but the foll instruction must be changed from "Rep rows 1-26 once more" to "Rep rows 1-23 once more". Omit "Rep rows 1-10 once more" *(49 rows)*.

stars and stripes

Designers are often asked to look at an existing logo, which in many cases has been in use for a long time, and they are commissioned to revamp the image. For this afghan I decided to look again at the familiar shape of the star. This motif is recognized throughout the world and has a variety of connotations. Some countries use it as a national symbol, while for many cultures it has religious significance. It has associations with astrology and navigation, and it is also used as a mark of excellence. Its regular, symmetrical outline makes it an easy and pleasing shape to interpret in knitting. I have combined glass beads with brightly colored matte cotton yarns to give the star motifs added sparkle. And I have enjoyed experimenting with the potential of reverse stockinette (stocking) stitch. As an alternative, the three striped squares in this design could be knitted in plain stockinette (stocking) stitch to give a totally different effect. Why not experiment yourself?

SIZE
85in × 59in (214cm × 148cm)

MATERIALS
1 pair US 5 (3.75mm/No. 9) needles
2 circular US 3 (3.25mm/No. 10)
   needles 39in (100cm) length

Yarn
Rowan Handknit DK Cotton
1¾oz (50g) balls

navy blue	9
cream	9
green	14
pale yellow	5
bright blue	5
red	6
khaki green	3
deep red	2

Quantities given for individual squares are approximate fractions of a ball.

Beads
³⁄₁₆in (5mm) pebble beads

pearl	728
silver	418
blue	608
red	613

Buttons
Green ceramic buttons	12

GAUGE (TENSION)
22 sts and 30 rows to 4in (10cm) measured over reverse stockinette (stocking) stitch using US 5 (3.75mm/No. 9) needles.

NOTE
Single stitch outlines on squares ⑧③ and ⑧⑤ can be Swiss-darned after knitting (see page 123).

ABBREVIATIONS
See also page 127.

FINISHING
The sizes given for the finished afghan and individual squares are approximate. The number of stitches in a row, and the number of rows in a square differ in some instances. Therefore, when sewing pieces together, ease the extra stitches or extra rows into the adjoining square.

Press the individual squares using a damp cloth and warm iron. Sew the squares together, joining bound (cast) off edge of one square to the cast on edge of the next square, easing in stitches if necessary, to form vertical strips. Sew the vertical strips together, easing in rows if necessary, to create one block.

Edging

MATERIALS

2 circular US 3 (3.25mm/No. 10) needles 39in (100cm) length

Yarn

Rowan Handknit DK Cotton
1¾oz (50g) balls
    green   1³⁄₅

Beads

³⁄₁₆in (5mm) pebble beads
    red   82
    blue   80
    pearl   162

KNIT

Thread on beads in 24 repeats of 1 red, 1 pearl, 1 blue, 1 pearl, ending with 1 red bead.
With RS facing, pick up and knit 481 sts along the right-hand edge of the afghan.
Beg with a WS row, work 4 rows in garter stitch (knit every row), inc 1 st at each end of RS rows *(485 sts)*.
NEXT ROW (WS): **Purl.**

NEXT ROW (RS): inc once into first st, K1, (pb red, K4, pb pearl, K4, pb blue, K4, pb pearl, K4) 24 times, pb red, inc once into next st, K1.
Work 2 rows in garter stitch, inc 1 st at each end of RS row.
Bind (cast) off sts knitwise.
Rep for left-hand edge of afghan.
Thread on 1 pearl bead and then 16 repeats of 1 red, 1 pearl, 1 blue, 1 pearl beads. With RS facing, pick up and knit 315 sts along bottom edge of the afghan.
Beg with a WS row, work 4 rows in garter stitch, inc 1 st at each end of RS rows *(319 sts)*.
NEXT ROW (WS): **Purl.**
NEXT ROW (RS): inc once into first st, K3, (pb pearl, K4, pb blue, K4, pb pearl, K4, pb red, K4) 15 times, pb pearl, K4, pb blue, K4, pb pearl, K2, inc in next st, K1.
Work 2 rows in garter stitch, inc 1 st at each end of RS row.
Bind (cast) off sts knitwise.
Rep for top edge of afghan.
Neatly sew border edges together.

Order of squares

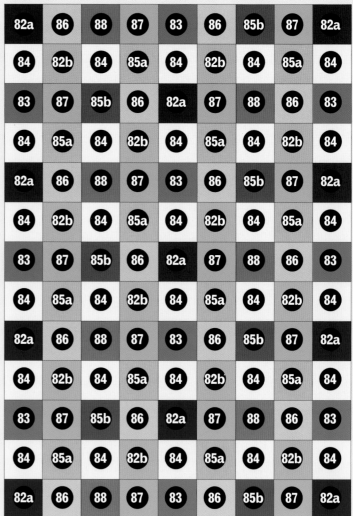

QUANTITY OF SQUARES

⑧²	Beaded star	
	⑧²ᵃ First colorway	11
	⑧²ᵇ Second colorway	12
⑧³	Twinkle	10
⑧⁴	Lime stripe	30
⑧⁵	Embossed star	
	⑧⁵ᵃ First colorway	12
	⑧⁵ᵇ Second colorway	7
⑧⁶	Multi-stripe	14
⑧⁷	Navy and white	14
⑧⁸	Super star	7

82 Beaded star

SIZE
6½in × 6½in (16.5cm × 16.5cm)

MATERIALS
1 pair US 5 (3.75mm/No. 9) needles

82a First colorway (×11 ⊞ ▣)
Rowan Handknit DK Cotton
1¾oz (50g) balls

■ navy blue	⅓

³⁄₁₆in (5mm) pebble beads

⊙ pearl	44
⊙ silver	38

☐ K on RS, P on WS

82b Second colorway (×12 ▣)
Rowan Handknit DK Cotton
1¾oz (50g) balls

green	⅓

³⁄₁₆in (5mm) pebble beads

blue	44
red	38

KNIT
Cast on 37 sts and work until
chart row 50 completed.
Bind (cast) off sts.

82a

82b

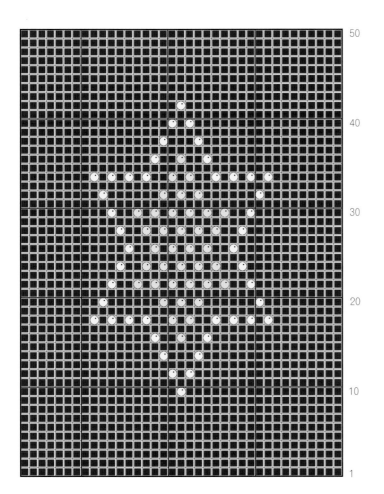

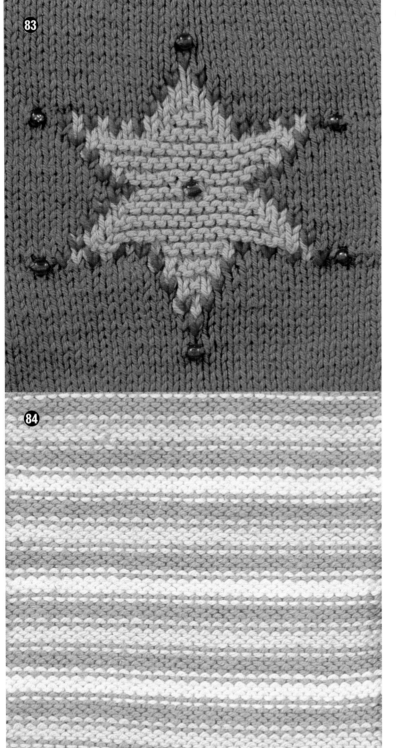

⑧③ Twinkle

SIZE
6½in × 6½in (16.5cm × 16.5cm)

MATERIALS
1 pair US 5 (3.75mm/No. 9) needles

Single colorway (×10 ⊞ ▣)
Rowan Handknit DK Cotton
1¾oz (50g) balls

■	bright blue	⅕
■	red	1/25
■	green	⅙

³⁄₁₆in (5mm) pebble beads
● red   7

□ K on RS, P on WS

⊟ P on RS, K on WS

KNIT
Cast on 37 sts and work until chart row 50 completed. Bind (cast) off sts.

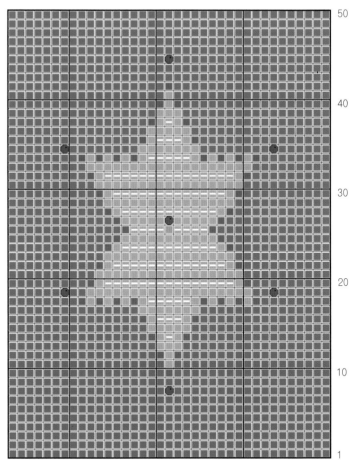

84 Lime stripe

SIZE
6½in × 6½in (16.5cm × 16.5cm)

MATERIALS
1 pair US 5 (3.75mm/No. 9) needles

Single colorway (×30 ■)
Rowan Handknit DK Cotton
1¾oz (50g) balls
cream (A)	⅒
green (B)	⅙
pale yellow (C)	⅒

KNIT
Cast on 38 sts using A.
Working in reverse stockinette
(stocking) stitch (purl on RS rows
and knit on WS rows), and beg
with a RS row, cont in stripe patt
rep as folls:
ROWS 1-3: **A.**
ROWS 4-6: **B.**
ROWS 7-9: **C.**
ROWS 10-12: **B.**
Rep rows 1-12, 3 times more.
Rep rows 1-3 once more.
(51 rows)
Bind (cast) off sts.

85 Embossed star

SIZE
6½in × 6½in (16.5cm × 16.5cm)

MATERIALS
1 pair US 5 (3.75mm/No. 9) needles

85a First colorway (×12 ⊞ ■)
Rowan Handknit DK Cotton
1¾oz (50g) balls
▦	khaki green (A)	⅕
▦	red (B)	⅕
▦	bright blue (C)	¹⁄₅₀

⊠ Green ceramic buttons 1

☐ K on RS, P on WS

⊟ P on RS, K on WS

85b Second colorway (×7 ■)
Rowan Handknit DK Cotton
1¾oz (50g) balls
deep red (A)	⅕
bright blue (B)	⅕
green (C)	¹⁄₅₀

Note: this colorway has no button.

KNIT
Cast on 37 sts and work until
chart row 50 completed.
Bind (cast) off sts.

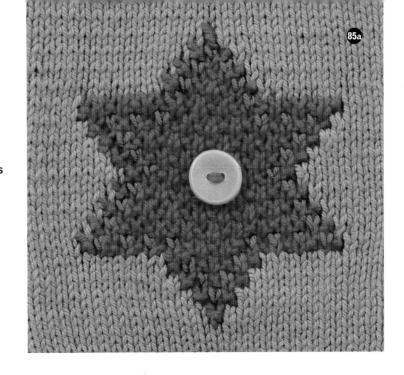

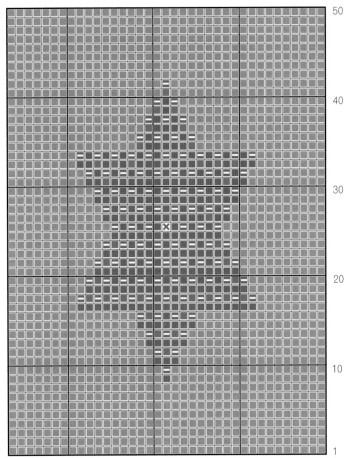

86 Multi-stripe

SIZE
6½in × 6½in (16.5cm × 16.5cm)

MATERIALS
1 pair US 5 (3.75mm/No. 9) needles

Single colorway (×14 ▣)
Rowan Handknit DK Cotton
1¾oz (50g) balls
cream (A)	⅕
red (B)	⅒
bright blue (C)	⅒

KNIT
Cast on 38 sts using A. Working in reverse stockinette (stocking) stitch (purl on RS rows and knit on WS rows), and beg with a RS row, cont in stripe patt rep as folls:
ROWS 1-3: **A.**
ROWS 4-6: **B.**
ROWS 7-9: **A.**
ROWS 10-12: **C.**
Rep rows 1-12, 3 times more.
Rep rows 1-3 once more.
(51 rows)
Bind (cast) off sts.

87 Navy and white

SIZE
6½in × 6½in (16.5cm × 16.5cm)

MATERIALS
1 pair US 5 (3.75mm/No. 9) needles

Single colorway (×14 ▣)
Rowan Handknit DK Cotton
1¾oz (50g) balls
navy blue (A)	⅕
cream (B)	⅙

KNIT
Cast on 38 sts using A. Working in reverse stockinette (stocking) stitch (purl on RS rows and knit on WS rows), and beg with a RS row, cont in stripe patt rep as folls:
ROWS 1-3: **A.**
ROWS 4-6: **B.**
Rep rows 1-6, 7 times more.
Rep rows 1-3 once more.
(51 rows)
Bind (cast) off sts.

88 Super star

SIZE
6½in × 6½in (16.5cm × 16.5cm)

MATERIALS
1 pair US 5 (3.75mm/No. 9) needles

Single colorway (×7 ⊞ ▣)
Rowan Handknit DK Cotton
1¾oz (50g) balls

◼	red	⅕
◼	bright blue	⅟₁₆
◼	navy blue	⅛

³⁄₁₆in (5mm) pebble beads

| ⊙ | pearl | 12 |
| ● | red | 1 |

☐ K on RS, P on WS

⊟ P on RS, K on WS

KNIT
Cast on 37 sts and work until chart row 50 completed. Bind (cast) off sts.

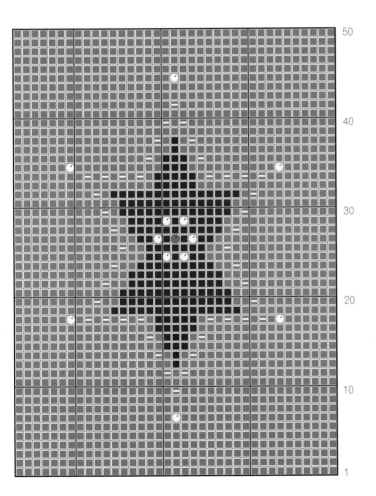

magic carpet

Inspired by an ancient Tunisian rug displayed on the wall of a hotel lobby, I eagerly made several sketches to record my initial ideas for what was to become Magic Carpet. The bold geometric shapes composed of zig-zags, chevrons and tessellated squares in strong colors lent themselves readily to my own way of working. I wanted this design to epitomize my whole experience of Tunisia – extreme heat, the foreign nature of the locality, the bustle of the crowded souks, the colorful spices and rich perfumes that permeated the dusty air. This was the first time that I used sequins in one of my designs, opening up a whole new area for me in handknitting. The myriad of colors reflected by the sequins, together with beads and bright yarns combine to evoke the exotic effects that I remember from my stay in North Africa. This afghan has a different edging that is fun to do: lengths of colored yarns are pulled through the edging of the afghan to form decorative tassels, thus creating a "Magic Carpet."

SIZE
56in × 56in (142cm × 142cm)

MATERIALS
1 pair US 5 (3.75mm/No. 9) needles
2 circular US 3 (3.25mm/No. 10) needles 39in (100cm) length
1 rug hook

Yarn
Rowan Wool Cotton
1¾oz (50g) balls

green	10
red	6
royal blue	7
magenta	6
pale yellow	7

Rowan Lurex Shimmer
(Used double throughout)
1oz (25g) balls

wine red	4
gold	3

Rowan Kidsilk Haze
(Used triple throughout)
1oz (25g) balls

orange	4
deep magenta	3

Beads
³⁄₁₆in (5mm) pebble beads

blue	456

Sequins
⁵⁄₁₆in (8mm) sequins

blue	1149
red	738
green	817
pink	1178

GAUGE (TENSION)
24 sts and 32 rows to 4 in (10cm) measured over patterned stockinette (stocking) stitch using US 5 (3.75mm/No. 9) needles.

NOTE
Single stitch outlines on squares ⑨⓪ ⑨① ⑨⑥ ⑨⑦ ⑨⑧ and ⑨⑨ can be Swiss-darned after knitting (see page 123).

ABBREVIATIONS
See also page 127.

FINISHING
The sizes given for the finished afghan and individual squares are approximate. The number of stitches in a row, and the number of rows in a square differ in some instances. Therefore, when sewing pieces together, ease the extra stitches or extra rows into the adjoining square.

Press the individual squares using a damp cloth and warm iron. Sew the squares together, joining bound (cast) off edge of one square to the cast on edge of the next square, easing in stitches if necessary, to form vertical strips. Sew the vertical strips together, easing in rows if necessary, to create one block.

Edging

MATERIALS

2 circular US 3 (3.25mm/No. 10)
    needles 39in (100cm) length
1 rug hook

Yarn

Rowan Wool Cotton
1¾oz (50g) balls
    red   1⅕

KNIT

With RS facing, pick up and knit
335 sts along the right-hand edge
of the afghan.

NEXT ROW (WS): Knit

NEXT ROW (RS): Inc once into first
st, K to last 2 sts, inc once into
next st, K1 *(337 sts)*.

NEXT ROW (WS) (EYELETS): K1, (yf,
K2tog) to end of row.

NEXT ROW (RS): Inc once into first
st, K to last 2 sts, inc once into
next st, K1 *(339 sts)*.

NEXT ROW (WS): Knit

NEXT ROW (RS): Inc once into first
st, K to last 2 sts, inc once into
next st, K1 *(341 sts)*.

Cast off sts knitwise.

Rep for left-hand edge of afghan.

With RS facing, pick up and
knit 331 sts along bottom edge of
the afghan.

Rep edging as for right-hand and
left-hand edges.

Rep for top edge of afghan.

Neatly sew border edges together.

TASSLES

Rowan Wool Cotton
1¾oz (50g) balls
    red   ⅗
    royal blue   ⅗
    magenta   ⅗
    pale yellow   ⅗
    green   ⅗

Cut the yarn into 5in (13cm)
lengths. Take 3 lengths of the
same color yarn and fold in half to
make 6 strands. Push the rug
hook through an eyelet in the
border then place the rug hook
through the fold in the strands of
yarn and close latch over yarn.
Pull through eyelet while holding
the ends of the tassle. Using the
rug hook carefully pull the ends of
the tassle through the fold in the
yarn, and pull up tightly to secure.
Starting at one end of the afghan,
add tassles to the border, keeping
to the col sequence above.

RIGHT: *The tasselled border adds
an extra decorative element to
this beaded and sequinned throw.*

Order of squares

90b	92	89c	91	100	91	89d	92	90d
92	95a	99a	99b	99c	99b	99a	95b	92
89b	96a	90b	92	89a	92	90d	97a	89b
91	96b	92	93b	98d	94b	92	97b	91
100	96c	89d	97d	90a	96d	89c	97c	100
91	96b	92	94a	99d	93a	92	97b	91
89a	96a	90a	92	89b	92	90c	97a	89a
92	95a	98a	98b	98c	98b	98a	95b	92
90a	92	89c	91	100	91	89d	92	90c

QUANTITY OF SQUARES

89 Shimmer
- 89a First colorway — 3
- 89b Second colorway — 3
- 89c Third colorway — 3
- 89d Fourth colorway — 3

90 Trinket box
- 90a First colorway — 3
- 90b Second colorway — 2
- 90c Third colorway — 2
- 90d Fourth colorway — 2

91 Grid — 8

92 Tunisian stripes — 16

93 Arabian stripes 1
- 93a First colorway — 1
- 93b Second colorway — 1

94 Arabian stripes 2
- 94a First colorway — 1
- 94b Second colorway — 1

95 Sparkle
- 95a First colorway — 2
- 95b Second colorway — 2

96 Aztec 1
- 96a First colorway — 2
- 96b Second colorway — 2
- 96c Third colorway — 1
- 96d Fourth colorway — 1

97 Aztec 2
- 97a First colorway — 2
- 97b Second colorway — 2
- 97c Third colorway — 1
- 97d Fourth colorway — 1

98 Aztec 3
- 98a First colorway — 2
- 98b Second colorway — 2
- 98c Third colorway — 1
- 98d Fourth colorway — 1

99 Aztec 4
- 99a First colorway — 2
- 99b Second colorway — 2
- 99c Third colorway — 1
- 99d Fourth colorway — 1

100 Sequin stripe — 4

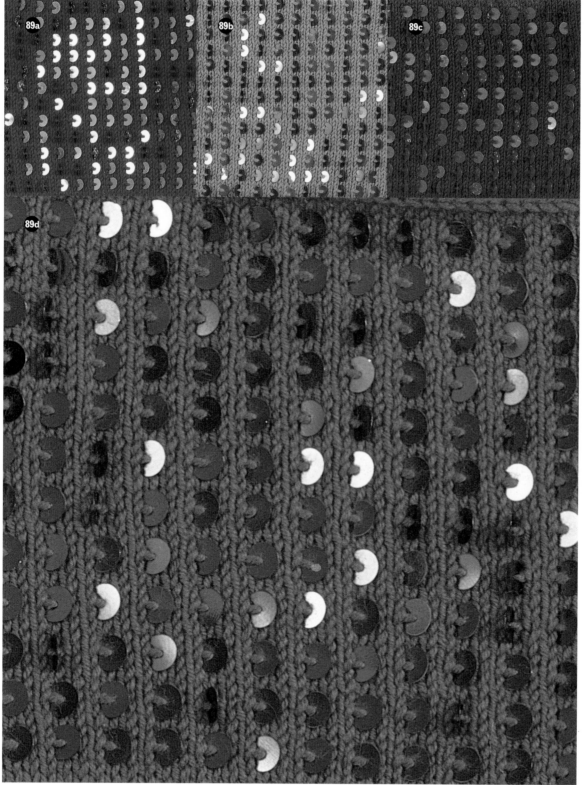

⑧⑨ Shimmer

SIZE
6¼in × 6¼in (15.5cm × 15.5cm)

MATERIALS
1 pair US 5 (3.75mm/No. 9) needles

⁸⁹ᵃ First colorway (×3 ■)
Rowan Wool Cotton
1¾oz (50g) balls
  red   ½

⁵⁄₁₆in (8mm) sequins
  green   156

⁸⁹ᵇ Second colorway (×3 ■)
Rowan Wool Cotton
1¾oz (50g) balls
  green   ½

⁵⁄₁₆in (8mm) sequins
  red   156

⁸⁹ᶜ Third colorway (×3 ■)
Rowan Wool Cotton
1¾oz (50g) balls
  royal blue   ½

⁵⁄₁₆in (8mm) sequins
  pink   156

⁸⁹ᵈ Fourth colorway (×3 ■)
Rowan Wool Cotton
1¾oz (50g) balls
  magenta   ½

⁵⁄₁₆in (8mm) sequins
  blue   156

KNIT
Thread on sequins.
Cast on 39 sts. Work 2 rows in stockinette (stocking) stitch.
ROW 3 (RS): K3, (ps, K2) to last 3 sts, ps, K2.
ROW 4 -6: Work 3 rows in stockinette (stocking) stitch.
Rep rows 3-6, 11 times more.
Rep rows 3-4 once more. (52 rows)
Bind (cast) off sts.

90 Trinket box

SIZE
6¼in × 6¼in (15.5cm × 15.5cm)

MATERIALS
1 pair US 5 (3.75mm/No. 9) needles

90a First colorway (×3 ▦ ▣)
Rowan Wool Cotton
1¾oz (50g) balls

▣ green (A)	⅛
■ red (B)	⅛
□ pale yellow (C)	½5
■ royal blue (D)	⅛
■ magenta (E)	⅛

⁵⁄₁₆in (8mm) sequins

● red (on A)	30
● green (on B)	30
● pink (on D)	30
● blue (on E)	30

☐ K on RS, P on WS

90b Second colorway (×2)
Rowan Wool Cotton
1¾oz (50g) balls

magenta (A)	⅛
royal blue (B)	⅛
pale yellow (C)	½5
red (D)	⅛
green (E)	⅛

⁵⁄₁₆in (8mm) sequins

blue (on A)	30
pink (on B)	30
green (on D)	30
red (on E)	30

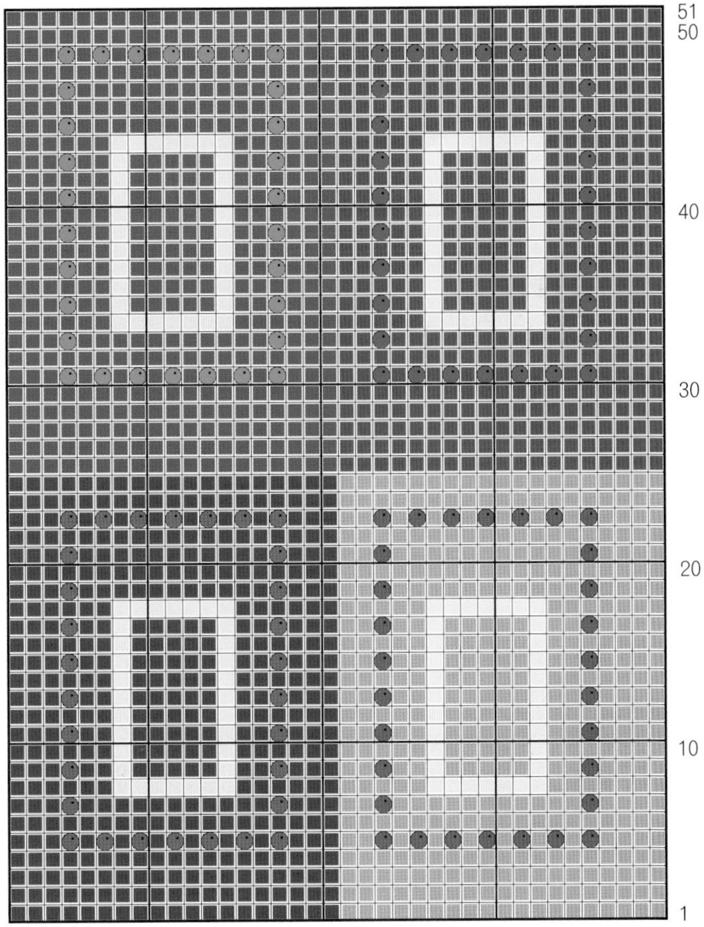

90c Third colorway (×2 ▣)
Rowan Wool Cotton
1¾oz (50g) balls

red (A)	⅛
green (B)	⅛
pale yellow (C)	½5
magenta (D)	⅛
royal blue (E)	⅛

⁵⁄₁₆in (8mm) sequins

green (on A)	30
red (on B)	30
blue (on D)	30
pink (on E)	30

90d Fourth colorway (×2)
Rowan Wool Cotton
1¾oz (50g) balls

royal blue (A)	⅛
magenta (B)	⅛
pale yellow (C)	½5
green (D)	⅛
red (E)	⅛

⁵⁄₁₆in (8mm) sequins

pink (on A)	30
blue (on B)	30
red (on D)	30
green (on E)	30

KNIT
Thread on sequins.
Cast on 38 sts and work until chart row 51 completed.
Bind (cast) off sts.

⑨ Grid

SIZE
6¼in × 6¼in (15.5cm × 15.5cm)

MATERIALS
1 pair US 5 (3.75mm/No. 9) needles

Single colorway (×8 ⊞ ◼)
Rowan Wool Cotton
1¾oz (50g) balls

◼ green	⅛
☐ pale yellow	⅛
◼ royal blue	1⁄12
◼ magenta	1⁄25

Rowan Lurex Shimmer
(Used double throughout)
1oz (25g) balls

◼ wine red	⅛
☐ gold	1⁄12

Rowan Kidsilk Haze
(Used triple throughout)
1oz (25g) balls

◼ orange	⅙
◼ deep magenta	1⁄12

☐ K on RS, P on WS

KNIT
Cast on 38 sts and work until chart row 50 completed. Bind (cast) off sts.

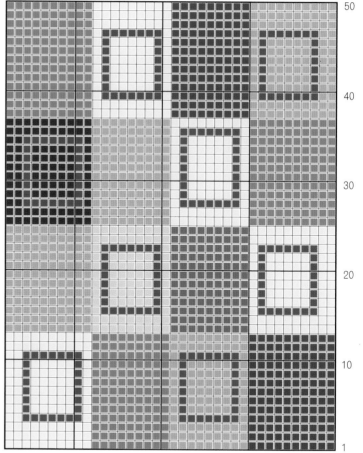

92 Tunisian stripes

SIZE

6¼in × 6¼in (15.5cm × 15.5cm)

MATERIALS

1 pair US 5 (3.75mm/No. 9) needles

Single colorway (×16 ▣)

Rowan Wool Cotton
1¾oz (50g) balls

green (A)	⅛
pale yellow (C)	1/10

Rowan Lurex Shimmer
(Used double throughout)
1oz (25g) balls

wine red (D)	1/25

Rowan Kidsilk Haze
(Used triple throughout)
1oz (25g) balls

orange (B)	⅛
deep magenta (E)	⅛

KNIT

Cast on 39 sts using A.
Working in stockinette (stocking) stitch (knit 1 row, purl 1 row), cont in stripe patt rep as folls, beg with a RS row:

ROWS 1-3: A.
ROWS 4-7: B.
ROWS 8-10: C.
ROWS 11-13: A.
ROW 14: D.
ROWS 15-16: E.
ROW 17: D.
ROWS 18-20: C.
Rep rows 1-20 once more.
Rep rows 1-10 once more.
(50 rows)
Bind (cast) off sts.

93 Arabian stripes 1

SIZE

6¼in × 6¼in (15.5cm × 15.5cm)

MATERIALS

1 pair US 5 (3.75mm/No. 9) needles

93a First colorway (×1 ⊞ ▣)

Rowan Wool Cotton
1¾oz (50g) balls

■ magenta (A)	1/10
■ green (B)	1/10
■ royal blue (C)	1/10

5/16in (8mm) sequins

● green (on A)	20
● blue (on B)	20
● pink (on C)	23

□ K on RS, P on WS

93b Second colorway (×1 ▣)

Rowan Wool Cotton
1¾oz (50g) balls

green (A)	1/10
magenta (B)	1/10
royal blue (C)	1/10

5/16in (8mm) sequins

blue (on A)	20
green (on B)	20
pink (on C)	23

KNIT

Thread on sequins.
Cast on 40 sts and work until chart row 50 completed.
Bind (cast) off sts.

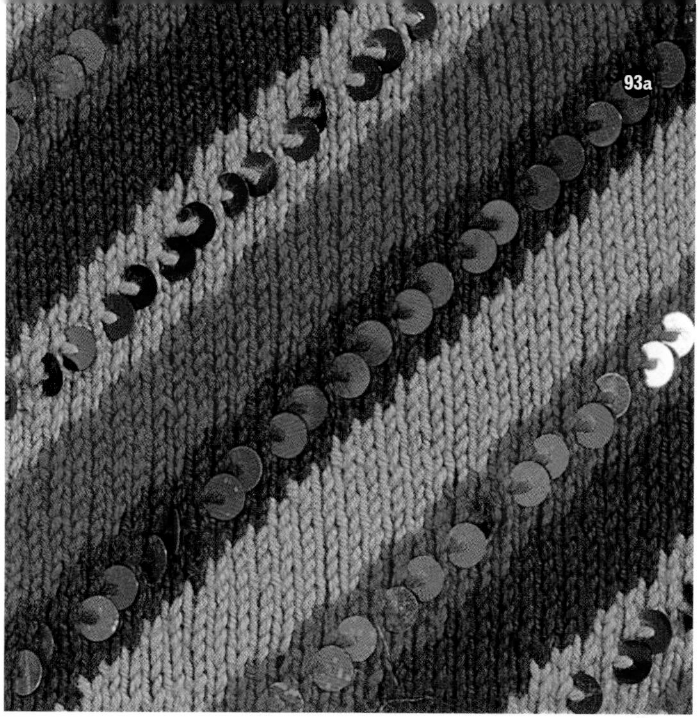

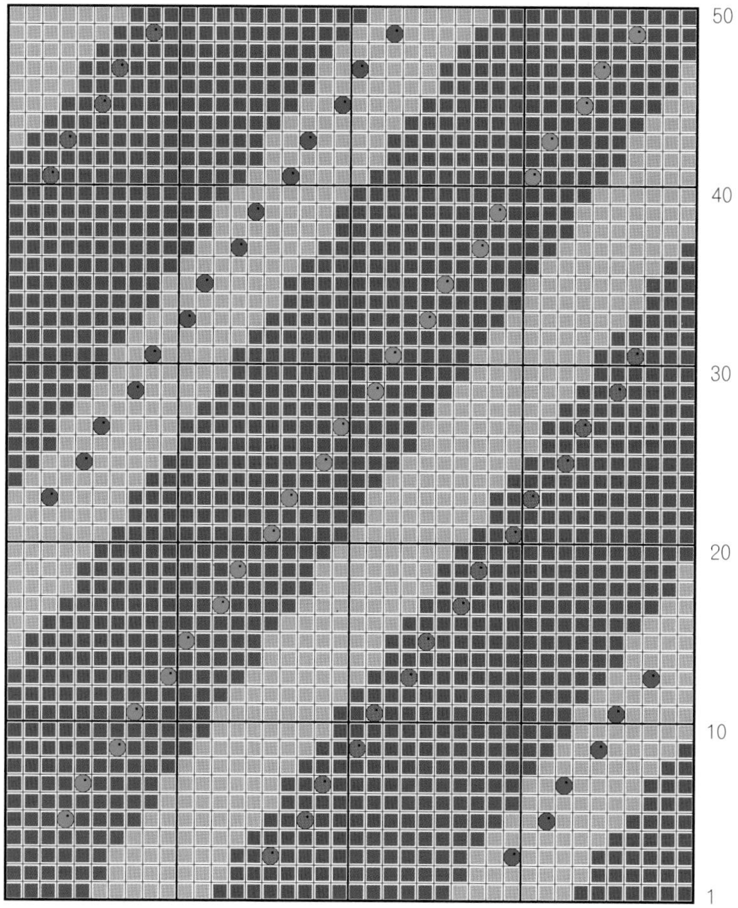

❾❹ Arabian stripes 2

□ K on RS, P on WS

SIZE

6¼in × 6¼in (15.5cm × 15.5cm)

MATERIALS

1 pair US 5 (3.75mm/No. 9) needles

❾❹ₐ First colorway (×1 ⊞ ▣)

Rowan Wool Cotton
1¾oz (50g) balls

- ■ royal blue (A)   ⅒
- ▢ green (B)   ⅒
- ■ magenta (C)   ⅒

⁵⁄₁₆in (8mm) sequins

- ● pink (on A)   23
- ● blue (on B)   19
- ● green (on C)   20

❾❹ᵦ Second colorway (×1 ▣)

Rowan Wool Cotton
1¾oz (50g) balls

- royal blue (A)   ⅒
- magenta (B)   ⅒
- green (C)   ⅒

⁵⁄₁₆in (8mm) sequins

- pink (on A)   23
- green (on B)   19
- blue (on C)   20

KNIT

Thread on sequins.
Cast on 40 sts and work until
chart row 50 completed.
Bind (cast) off sts.

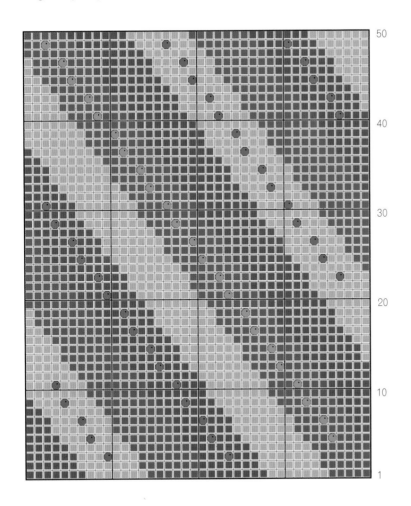

⑨⑤ Sparkle

SIZE
6¼in × 6¼in (15.5cm × 15.5cm)

MATERIALS
1 pair US 5 (3.75mm/No. 9) needles

⑨⁵ᵃ First colorway (×2 ⊞ ▣)
Rowan Wool Cotton
1¾oz (50g) balls

■ royal blue (A)	⅛
▨ green (B)	⅛
■ red (C)	⅛
□ pale yellow (D)	⅛

⁵⁄₁₆in (8mm) sequins

● blue (on B)	51
◔ pink (on D)	51

□ K on RS, P on WS

⑨⁵ᵇ Second colorway (×2 ▣)
Rowan Wool Cotton
1¾oz (50g) balls

red (A)	⅛
green (B)	⅛
royal blue (C)	⅛
pale yellow (D)	⅛

⁵⁄₁₆in (8mm) sequins

blue (on B)	51
pink (on D)	51

KNIT
Thread on sequins.
Cast on 38 sts and work until
chart row 51 completed.
Bind (cast) off sts.

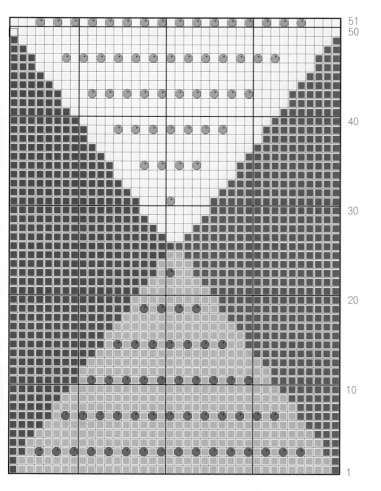

96 Aztec 1

SIZE

6¼in × 6¼in (15.5cm × 15.5cm)

MATERIALS

1 pair US 5 (3.75mm/No. 9) needles

96a First colorway (×2 ▦ ■)

Rowan Wool Cotton
1¾oz (50g) balls
- ■ magenta (A) ⅙
- ■ royal blue (B) ¹⁄₂₅
- ▨ green (C) ¹⁄₁₀

Rowan Lurex Shimmer
(Used double throughout)
1oz (25g) balls
- ■ wine red (D) ¹⁄₂₅

Rowan Kidsilk Haze
(Used triple throughout)
1oz (25g) balls
- ▨ orange (E) ⅙

³⁄₁₆in (5mm) pebble beads
- ● blue 19

□ K on RS, P on WS

96b Second colorway (×2 ■)

Rowan Wool Cotton
1¾oz (50g) balls
- royal blue (A) ⅙
- red (B) ¹⁄₂₅
- pale yellow (C) ¹⁄₁₀
- green (D) ¹⁄₅₀

Rowan Kidsilk Haze
(Used triple throughout)
1oz (25g) balls
- deep magenta (E) ⅙

³⁄₁₆in (5mm) pebble beads
- blue 19

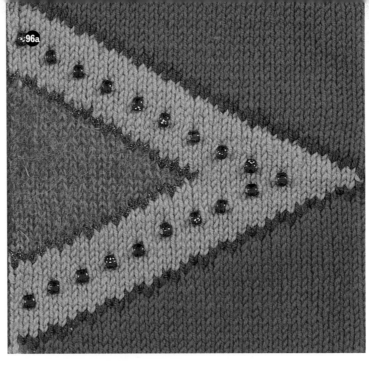

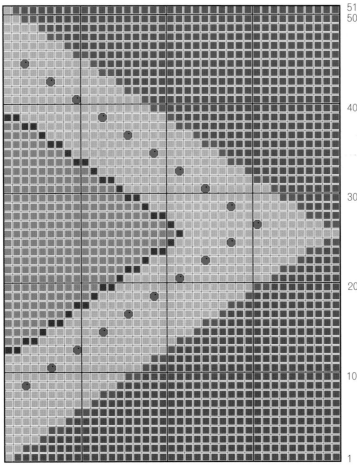

96c Third colorway (×1)

Rowan Wool Cotton
1¾oz (50g) balls
- green (A) ⅙
- magenta (C) ¹⁄₁₀
- royal blue (D) ¹⁄₅₀

Rowan Lurex Shimmer
(Used double throughout)
1oz (25g) balls
- wine red (B) ¹⁄₁₂
- gold (E) ⅙

³⁄₁₆in (5mm) pebble beads
- blue 19

96d Fourth colorway (×1)

Rowan Wool Cotton
1¾oz (50g) balls
- pale yellow (A) ⅙
- royal blue (B) ¹⁄₂₅
- red (C) ¹⁄₁₀
- green (D) ¹⁄₅₀

Rowan Lurex Shimmer
(Used double throughout)
1oz (25g) balls
- gold (E) ⅙

³⁄₁₆in (5mm) pebble beads
- blue 19

KNIT

Thread beads onto C.
Cast on 39 sts and work until
chart row 51 completed.
Bind (cast) off sts.

97 Aztec 2

SIZE
6¼in × 6¼in (15.5cm × 15.5cm)

MATERIALS
1 pair US 5 (3.75mm/No. 9) needles

97a First colorway (×2 ⊞)
Rowan Wool Cotton
1¾oz (50g) balls

green (A)	1/10
royal blue (B)	1/25
magenta (C)	1/6

Rowan Lurex Shimmer
(Used double throughout)
1oz (25g) balls

wine red (D)	1/25

Rowan Kidsilk Haze
(Used triple throughout)
1oz (25g) balls

orange (E)	1/6

3/16in (5mm) pebble beads

● blue	19

□ K on RS, P on WS

97b Second colorway (×2 ■)
Rowan Wool Cotton
1¾oz (50g) balls

pale yellow (A)	1/10
red (B)	1/25
royal blue (C)	1/6
green (D)	1/50

Rowan Kidsilk Haze
(Used triple throughout)
1oz (25g) balls

deep magenta (E)	1/6

3/16in (5mm) pebble beads

blue	19

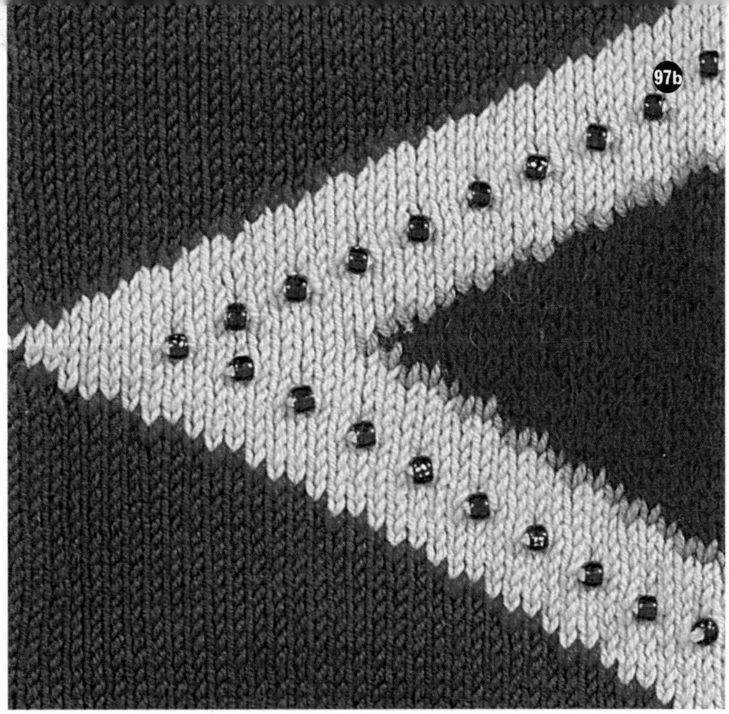

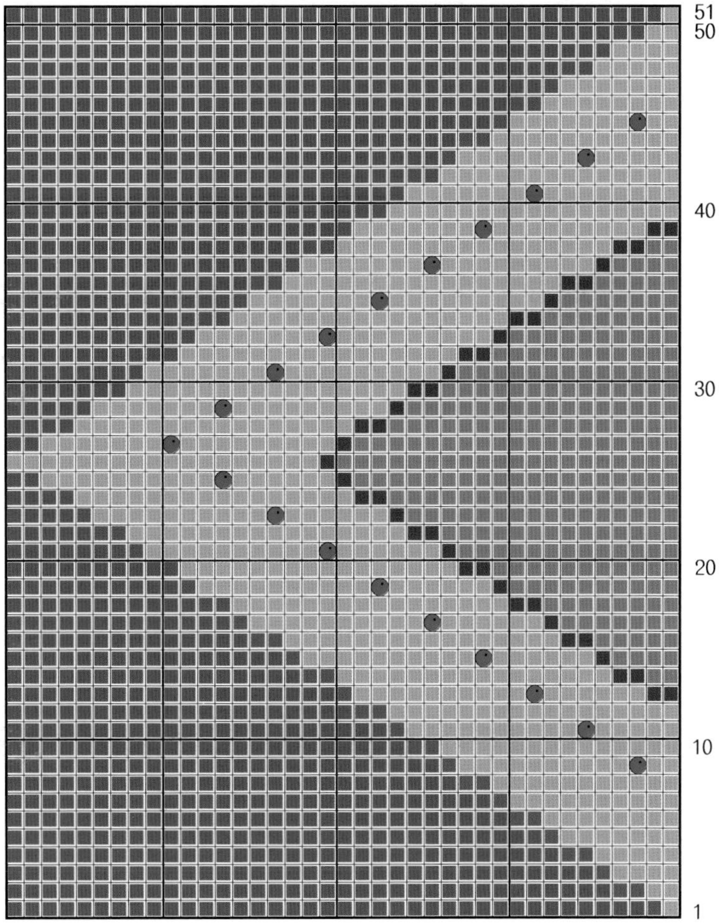

97c Third colorway (×1)
Rowan Wool Cotton
1¾oz (50g) balls

magenta (A)	1/10
green (C)	1/6
royal blue (D)	1/50

Rowan Lurex Shimmer
(Used double throughout)
1oz (25g) balls

wine red (B)	1/12
gold (E)	1/6

3/16in (5mm) pebble beads

blue	19

97d Fourth colorway (×1)
Rowan Wool Cotton
1¾oz (50g) balls

red (A)	1/10
royal blue (B)	1/25
pale yellow (C)	1/6
green (D)	1/50

Rowan Lurex Shimmer
(Used double throughout)
1oz (25g) balls

gold (E)	1/6

3/16in (5mm) pebble beads

blue	19

KNIT
Thread beads onto A.
Cast on 39 sts and work until chart row 51 completed.
Bind (cast) off sts.

98 Aztec 3

SIZE
6¼in × 6¼in (15.5cm × 15.5cm)

MATERIALS
1 pair US 5 (3.75mm/No. 9) needles

98a First colorway (×2 ⊞)
Rowan Wool Cotton
1¾oz (50g) balls
- ■ royal blue (A) 1/25
- ■ green (B) 1/10
- ■ magenta (E) 1/6

Rowan Lurex Shimmer
(Used double throughout)
1oz (25g) balls
- ■ wine red (C) 1/25

Rowan Kidsilk Haze
(Used triple throughout)
1oz (25g) balls
- ■ orange (D) 1/6

3/16in (5mm) pebble beads
- ● blue 19

□ K on RS, P on WS

98b Second colorway (×2)
Rowan Wool Cotton
1¾oz (50g) balls
- red (A) 1/25
- pale yellow (B) 1/10
- green (C) 1/50
- royal blue (E) 1/6

Rowan Kidsilk Haze
(Used triple throughout)
1oz (25g) balls
- deep magenta (D) 1/6

3/16in (5mm) pebble beads
- blue 19

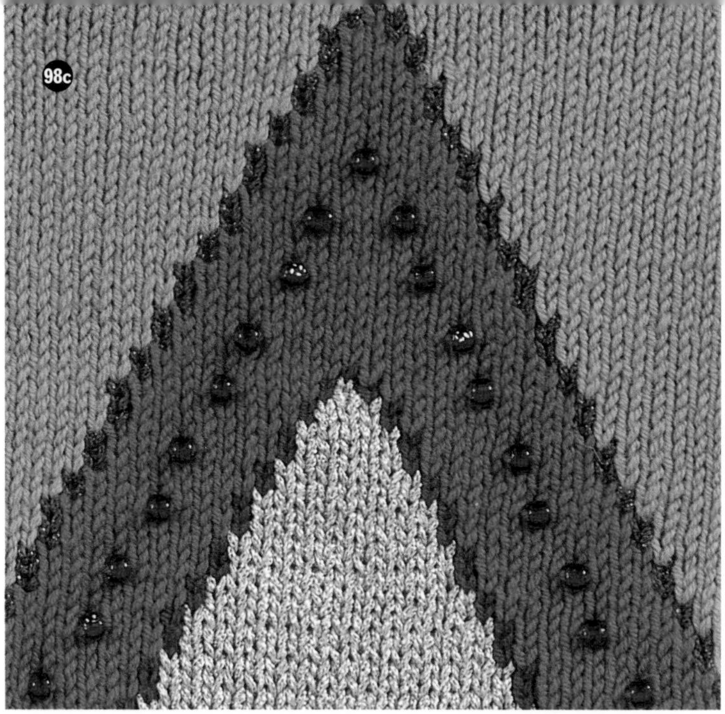

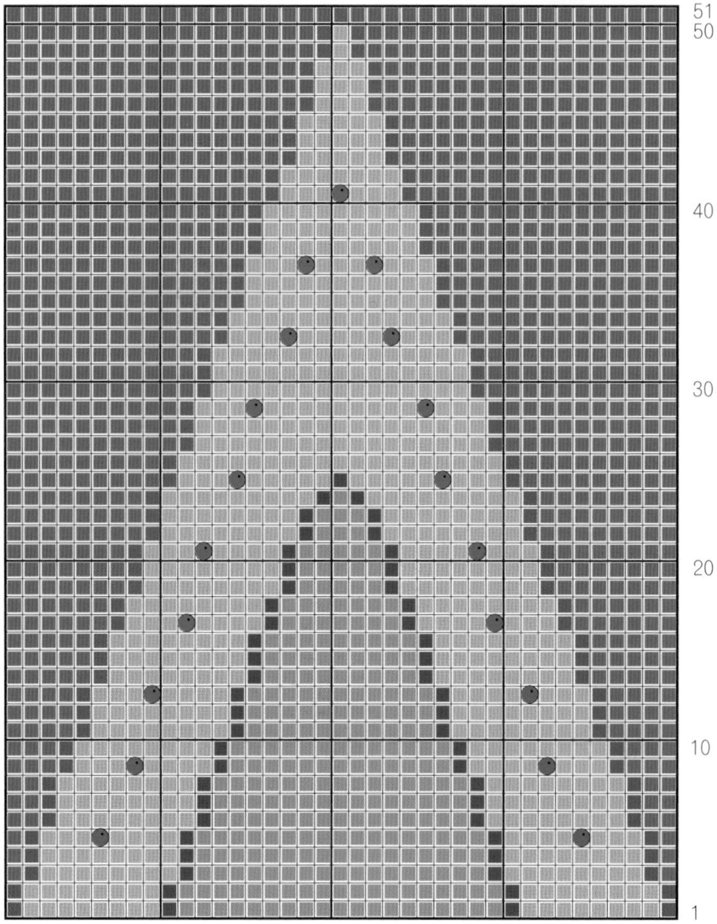

98c Third colorway (×1 ■)
Rowan Wool Cotton
1¾oz (50g) balls
- magenta (B) 1/10
- royal blue (C) 1/50
- green (E) 1/6

Rowan Lurex Shimmer
(Used double throughout)
1oz (25g) balls
- wine red (A) 1/12
- gold (D) 1/6

3/16in (5mm) pebble beads
- blue 19

98d Fourth colorway (×1)
Rowan Wool Cotton
1¾oz (50g) balls
- royal blue (A) 1/25
- red (B) 1/10
- green (C) 1/50
- pale yellow (E) 1/6

Rowan Lurex Shimmer
(Used double throughout)
1oz (25g) balls
- gold (D) 1/6

3/16in (5mm) pebble beads
- blue 19

KNIT
Thread beads onto B.
Cast on 39 sts and work until chart row 51 completed.
Bind (cast) off sts.

99 Aztec 4

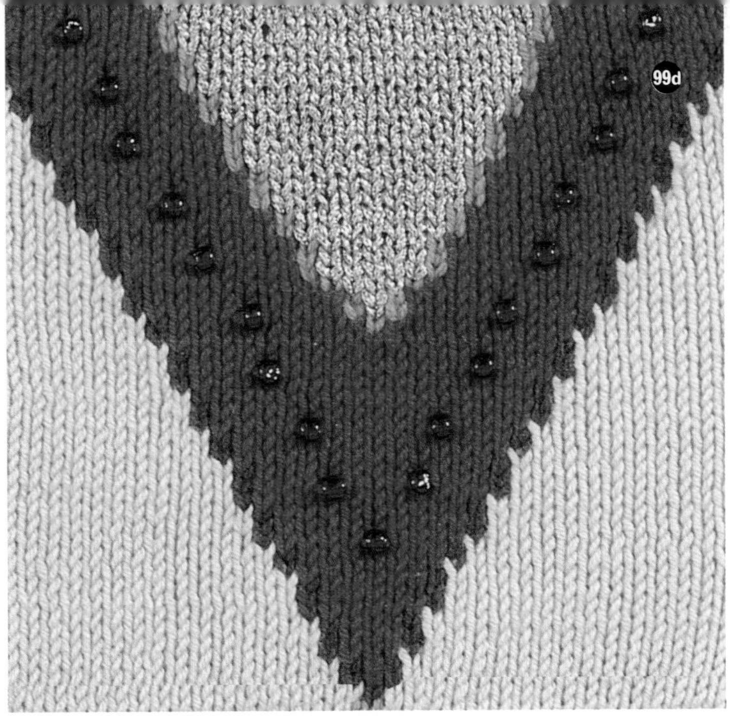

SIZE

6¼in × 6¼in (15.5cm × 15.5cm)

MATERIALS

1 pair US 5 (3.75mm/No. 9) needles

99a First colorway (×2 ⊞)

Rowan Wool Cotton
1¾oz (50g) balls
■ magenta (A) 1/6
■ royal blue (B) 1/25
■ green (C) 1/10

Rowan Lurex Shimmer
(Used double throughout)
1oz (25g) balls
■ wine red (D) 1/25

Rowan Kidsilk Haze
(Used triple throughout)
1oz (25g) balls
■ orange (E) 1/6

3/16in (5mm) pebble beads
● blue 19

□ K on RS, P on WS

99b Second colorway (×2)

Rowan Wool Cotton
1¾oz (50g) balls
royal blue (A) 1/6
red (B) 1/25
pale yellow (C) 1/10
green (D) 1/50

Rowan Kidsilk Haze
(Used triple throughout)
1oz (25g) balls
deep magenta (E) 1/6

3/16in (5mm) pebble beads
blue 19

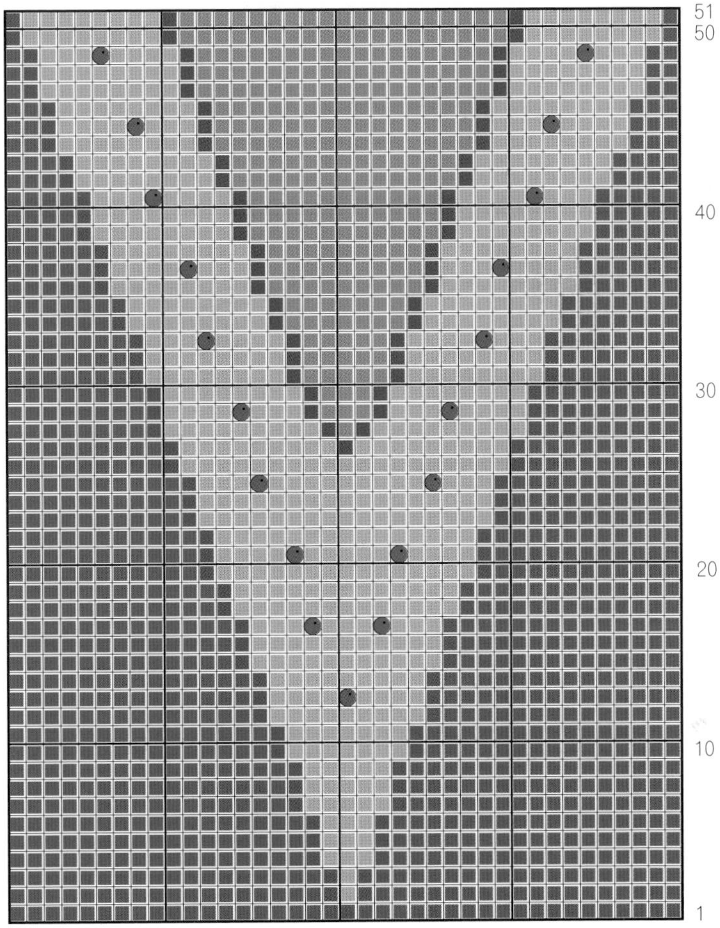

99c Third colorway (×1)

Rowan Wool Cotton
1¾oz (50g) balls
green (A) 1/6
magenta (C) 1/10
royal blue (D) 1/50

Rowan Lurex Shimmer
(Used double throughout)
1oz (25g) balls
wine red (B) 1/12
gold (E) 1/6

3/16in (5mm) pebble beads
blue 19

99d Fourth colorway (×1 ■)

Rowan Wool Cotton
1¾oz (50g) balls
pale yellow (A) 1/6
royal blue (B) 1/25
red (C) 1/10
green (D) 1/50

Rowan Lurex Shimmer
(Used double throughout)
1oz (25g) balls
gold (E) 1/6

3/16in (5mm) pebble beads
blue 19

KNIT

Thread beads onto C.
Cast on 39 sts and work until chart row 51 completed.
Bind (cast) off sts.

⓽⓪ Sequin stripe

SIZE
6¼in × 6¼in (15.5cm × 15.5cm)

MATERIALS
1 pair US 5 (3.75mm/No. 9) needles

Single colorway (×4 ■)
Rowan Wool Cotton
1¾oz (50g) balls
    magenta (A)   ¹⁄₁₀
    green (C)   ⅛
    royal blue (D)   ¹⁄₁₆

Rowan Lurex Shimmer
(Used double throughout)
1oz (25g) balls
    gold (B)   ⅛

⁵⁄₁₆in (8mm) sequins
    pink   36
    blue   32

KNIT
Thread sequins onto C before
starting to knit in the foll
sequence: 1 pink, 1 blue, 1 pink,
1 blue, etc.
Cast on 38 sts using A.
Working in stockinette (stocking)
stitch (knit 1 row, purl 1 row), cont
in stripe patt rep as folls, beg with
a RS row:
ROWS 1-4: **A.**
ROW 5: **B.**
ROWS 6-8: **C.**
ROW 9 (RS): **C,** K3, (ps, K1, ps, K1)
until 3 sts rem, ps, K2.
ROW 10: **C.**
ROW 11: **B.**
ROWS 12-16: **D.**
ROW 17: **B.**
ROWS 18-20: **C.**
ROW 21 (RS): **C,** as row 9.
ROW 22: **C.**
ROW 23 : **B.**
ROWS 24-28: **A.**
Rep rows 5-27 once more.
(51 rows)
Bind (cast) off sts.

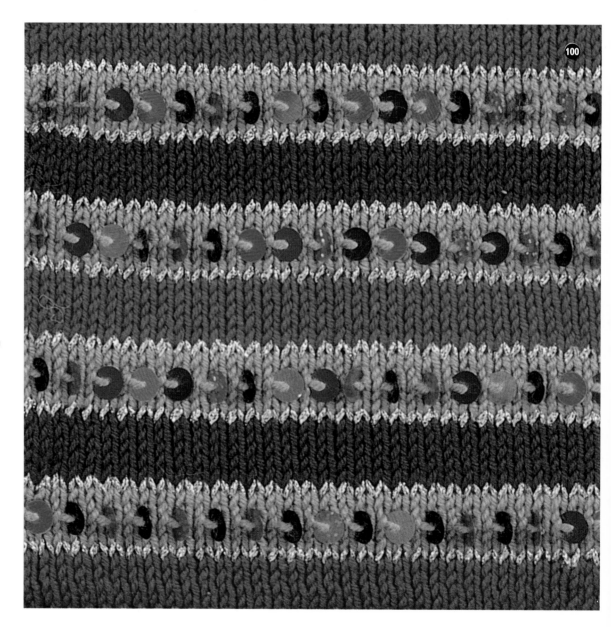

Techniques

INTARSIA KNITTING

Intarsia knitting produces a single thickness fabric that uses different balls of yarn for different areas of color. There should be very little, if any, carrying across of yarns at the back of the work.

There are several ways to help keep the separate colors of yarn organized while you are working. My preferred method is to use yarn bobbins. Small amounts of yarn can be wound onto bobbins, which should then be kept close to the back of the work while knitting, and only unwound when more yarn is needed.

Most of the intarsia patterns in this book are given in the form of a chart. It is advisable to make a color copy of the chart and to enlarge it if you prefer. This copy can be used as a worksheet on which rows can be marked off as they are worked and any notes can be made.

Joining in a new color

1 Insert the right needle into the next stitch. Place the end of the new pink yarn between the tips of the needles and across the blue yarn from left to right.

2 Take the new pink yarn under the blue yarn and knit the next stitch with it. Move the tail of pink yarn off the right needle as the new stitch is formed.

Changing colors

To avoid gaps between stitches when changing color, it is essential that the two yarns are crossed over at the back of the work.

1 On a knit row, insert the right needle into the next stitch. Place the old blue yarn over the new pink yarn. Pull the new pink yarn up and knit the stitch.

2 On a purl row, insert the right needle into the next stitch. Place the old pink yarn over the new blue yarn. Pull the new blue yarn up and purl the next stitch.

Darning in the ends

When an intarsia square is completed there will be loose ends to darn in on the back of the work.

1 Darn the ends around shapes of the same color by darning in one direction first.

2 Then darn the end back on itself, stretching the work before cutting the end of the yarn.

KNITTING WITH BEADS

There are many different types of bead available, but not all of them are suitable for hand-knitting. When choosing beads it is important to check that the bead hole is big enough for the yarn to pass through. In addition the weight and size of the beads also needs to be considered. For example, large heavy beads on 4-ply knitting will look clumsy and cause the fabric to sag. It is also wise to check whether the beads you are using are washable, as some may not be.

When you have chosen your beads, you are ready to thread them onto the yarn before you start to knit. There is a very easy way to do this:

Threading beads onto yarn

1 Place a length of sewing cotton beneath the yarn, then bring the two ends of the cotton together and thread both ends through a sewing needle.

2 Thread the beads onto the needle, then push them down the sewing cotton and onto the knitting yarn. Remember that the first bead you thread onto the yarn will be the last one to be knitted in.

Adding beads with a slip stitch

This is my preferred method of adding beads to knitting, and it works on both wrong side and right side rows. The beads sit in front of a slipped stitch, and hang down slightly from where they are knitted in. I have found that if the yarn is held quite firmly and the next stitch after the bead is knitted tightly, the bead sits very neatly and snugly against the knitting.

The following instructions show how to bead on a right side row: Work to where the bead is to be placed. Bring the yarn forward between the points of the needles.

1 Push a bead up the yarn to the front of the work, so that it rests in front of the right needle.

2 Slip the next stitch purlwise from the left to the right needle, leaving the bead in front of the slipped stitch.

3 Take the yarn between the needles to the back of the work and continue in pattern. The bead is now secured in position.

Adding beads on a wrong side row

When beads are placed on a wrong side row the instructions are almost the same. When a bead is to be added, take the yarn back between the needle points and push a bead up to the front of the work. Slip the next stitch exactly as above, but then bring the yarn forward and continue working.

KNITTING WITH SEQUINS

Although using sequins in hand-knitting has been practiced for many years, I only started to experiment with them while working on the Magic Carpet afghan. Some of the sequins that I have used are plain in color, but I also found some sequins that resemble mini holograms, and these create quite spectacular multi-colored effects when held in the light. Sequins not only add extra color and sparkle to a knitted fabric, but they also change the quality and feel of the knitting. The all-over sequinned squares in Magic Carpet feel like soft fish scales and create a very tactile piece of fabric.

When choosing sequins it is important to remember that the hole through the center must be big enough for the yarn to pass through. The size of the sequin should also be considered, and chosen in relation to the weight of yarn used. And, as with beads, it is also best to check if the sequins are washable before buying them.

The method of adding sequins to knitting is identical to the way that beads are knitted in. However, care should be taken to hold the sequins flat to the fabric while knitting, ensuring that they are all laying the same way. And it is advisable only to place sequins while working on a right side row, as it is extremely difficult to do this on a wrong side row.

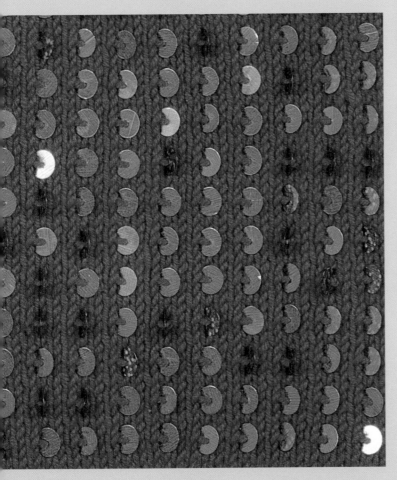

ADDING EMBROIDERY TO KNITTING

Outlines, single dots or fancy shapes and textures can be added to your fabric after knitting. It is advisable to finish knitting your square and tidy up the loose ends before embroidering. A large, blunt darning needle should be used to avoid splitting the stitches, and a yarn of the same or a slightly heavier weight as the main knitting that will easily cover the stitches is recommended.

I have used two basic embroidery stitches in the designs in this book. The first is Swiss-darning. This is a method of duplicating knitted stitches on plain stockinette (stocking) stitch fabrics using a needle and a separate length of yarn. It is a quick and easy way of adding dashes of color or outlines, and it can be worked horizontally or vertically.

Swiss-darning (worked horizontally)

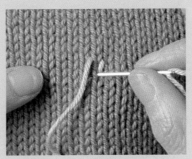

1 From the back of the work, insert the needle through the base of the knitted stitch, then take the needle around the top of the knitted stitch, as shown.

2 From the front of the work, insert the needle through the base of the same knitted stitch. Pull the yarn through. You have now covered a stitch.

Swiss-darning (worked vertically)

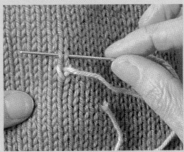

3 Bring the needle through the base of the next knitted stitch on the left, repeating steps 1–2 to form another complete stitch. Continue in this way.

1 Darn the first stitch, then bring the needle through the base of the stitch above the one just worked. Work that stitch in the same way. Continue forming the stitches as for horizontal darning, but work upwards rather than right to left.

The second embroidery technique is called Lazy Daisy stitch. This is a method of creating a decorative floral shape by working individual chain stitches in a group around a central point.

Lazy Daisy

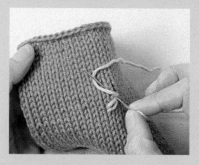 

1 From the front of the work, insert the needle through to the back of the work and out the front again, as shown. Loop the yarn around the needle's point.

2 Pull the yarn so that the loop lies flat across the fabric, then secure the tip of the loop with a small, straight stitch.

BLOCKING AND PRESSING

The blocking and pressing of knitted panels is an essential part of the finishing process, and one that is often omitted by knitters. There are several reasons why blocking and pressing should be done. Firstly, it flattens the edges of the knitting, which makes it easier to pick up stitches or sew together panels. Secondly, it ensures that the panels are of the correct measurement. And lastly, it finishes the knitted fabric, and in most cases changes the physical quality of the knitting, smoothing out stitches and making the fabric feel softer and more fluid.

Blocking is the pinning out of the knitted pieces, which should be done on a flat surface with the wrong side facing up. A tape measure should be used to ensure that the pieces are of the correct size. The temperature of the iron used for pressing is dependant on the fiber content of the yarn, as is the damp or dry pressing cloth, which must completely cover the panel that is going to be pressed. The general rule is as follows: natural fibers require a damp pressing cloth and a warm iron, and synthetic fibers and mixes require a dry pressing cloth and a cool iron. However, not all yarns conform to these rules and some have alternative requirements, so it is always advisable to read the pressing instructions that are printed on the ball band. If several different yarns have been used in one piece of knitting, it is better to play safe and follow the instructions for the most delicate yarn. If the heat of the iron is too hot, it could ruin the knitting permanently, resulting in a limp and lifeless piece of knitting that is irreversible.

After pressing it is best to leave the knitting pinned out for at least half an hour to allow all of the heat and moisture to evaporate. Then, when the pins are removed, the knitting will be flat and ready for sewing up.

PIECING TOGETHER YOUR AFGHAN

After spending many hours knitting the squares for your afghan it is very important that the sewing together of the squares is done as neatly as possible. I would recommend that mattress stitch is used, because it is easy to learn, very precise and it creates an almost invisible seam. One big advantage of using this stitch over other methods of sewing up is that you work with the right sides of the knitting facing up towards you, which enables you to see exactly how the seam is progressing.

A blunt sewing-up needle and a matching yarn should be used to sew together the squares. Lay the pieces of knitting out on a flat surface in the order in which they are to be pieced together. I would advise that the squares are sewn together to create vertical strips, then the vertical strips sewn together to create a block.

Mattress stitch seam (sewing stitches to stitches)

1 From the back of the work, insert the needle through the center of the first stitch along one of the edges, leaving a long tail of yarn.

2 From the back of the work, insert the needle between the first and the second stitches along the opposite edge.

3 Continue in this way, zigzagging backwards and forwards from edge to edge. Weave in the ends when you have completed the seam.